ONOMATOPEE

SUPERSTORM
DESIGN AND POLITICS IN THE AGE OF INFORMATION

NOEMI BIASETTON

ONOMATOPEE #243

AUTHOR
Noemi Biasetton

PROOFREADER
Robin Straaijer

COVER & ART DIRECTION
Michele Galluzzo

PUBLISHER
Onomatopee Projects,
Eindhoven (NL)
Jesse Muller and Natasha Rijkhoff

ISBN 978-90-833621-7-5
ONOMATOPEE #243

PRINTER
Elcograf S.p.A.

TYPEFACE
EB Garamond

I EDITION MARCH 2024
II EDITION JULY 2025
© NOEMI BIASETTON 2025

Every effort has been made to trace copyright holders and to obtain their permission for the use of copyright material.

All rights reserved. No part of this book may be reproduced in any form without permission from the author or publisher. To request permission, contact the author at www.noemibiasetton.com

The elements of the cover are a tribute to Area Cronica Entertainment, Mimmo Castellano, Luigi Ghirri, Aldo Novarese, Billy Lobo and Bronisław Zelek.

CONTENTS

PREFACE
This Boyfriend is Distracted
by Silvio Lorusso   11

INTRODUCTION   15

     Notes on the Superstorm   20
     On Reading the Superstorm   23
     Book Structure   29
     Research Considerations   31

1   GENEALOGY OF THE SUPERSTORM.
      NEW MEDIA, POLITICS, AND DESIGN   34

     Lights, Camera, Action   36
     Bad Media/Good Media   46
     Hope and Distrust   56
     Weather Report nr. 1   78

2   ANATOMY OF THE SUPERSTORM.
      DESIGN ISSUES IN A MEDIATIZED WORLD   82

     Agency and the Spectacle   86
     Re-imagining Mediation   100
     The Issue of Authorship   111
     Weather Report nr. 2   121

3 DESIGN AND THE SUPERSTORM. DESIGN *WITH* / *ABOUT* / *OF* POLITICS — 126

Design *with* Politics
    The 2008 Obama Campaign — 133
    The 2016 Clinton Logo — 143
Design *about* Politics
    Steve Bannon: A Propaganda Retrospective — 157
Design *of* Politics
    The Beast — 166
    Le Bimbe di Giuseppe Conte — 177
Weather Report nr. 3 — 190

CONCLUSIONS — 196

Old Weapons, New Struggles — 197
For a Post-Nostalgic Practice — 200
Weathering the Superstorm — 207

AUTHOR'S NOTE — 213

INDEX OF NAMES — 217
BIBLIOGRAPHY — 225

ACKNOWLEDGEMENTS — 243
ABOUT THE AUTHOR — 247

> Take a look at these hands
> Take a look at these hands
> The hand speaks
> The hand of a government man
> Well, I'm a tumbler
> Born under punches
> I'm so thin

BORN UNDER PUNCHES (THE HEAT GOES ON)
TALKING HEADS (1980)

"Hell is empty. And all the devils are here."

ARIEL IN *THE TEMPEST* (ACT I, SCENE 2)
WILLIAM SHAKESPEARE (1611)

To my dad

THIS BOYFRIEND IS DISTRACTED

We've all seen the stock photo. Its caption reads: "Disloyal man (known as Mario) walking with his girlfriend (Laura) and looking amazed at another seductive girl (name unknown)". Here is a possible symbolic reading of the scene: Mario represents Western politics; the red-dressed girl stands for new media technologies (particularly social media); and finally Laura is us, namely, communication designers.

The meme is a fitting allegory for the stalemate that Noemi Biasetton describes in this book. The liaison between politics and new media is becoming increasingly intimate, and it seems that all communication designers can do is watch, aghast. Well-crafted logos and visual identities alone won't win people's hearts – in fact, they might even lose them! For it is not so much the logo that matters, as the *discussion* surrounding the logo – 'discussion' being an euphemism for *crowdsmashing*, an online practice that seems to be politically agnostic.

This is not just a case of "bad publicity is good publicity". When Michael Bierut, a distinguished member of the professional design elite, mocks the typography of the MAGA hat for its bad kerning, he is completely missing the point. Designers are like fish unaware of the water, which is not a calm sea, but a multimedia and multi-modal tsunami. This is what Biasetton calls the Superstorm. In such a context, a communication designer shouldn't be surprised when the fandom's tributes to a prime minister appear on Pornhub (as it has happened with the Italian Giuseppe Conte). The phenomena caused by the Superstorm may appear silly and vulgar, but a winning political strategy doesn't know neither silliness nor vulgarity. While communication professionals ridicule the clumsiness, kitsch and plain bad taste of populist designs, the latter persevere, as they see bad taste, kitsch and clumsiness not as a vice but as a virtue. This is one of the lessons we learn from reading Biasetton's book.

The demise of the Madmen-style communication experts did not happen all of a sudden. As shown by the activity of Atelier Populaire – whose assemblies to pick posters to print were not that far removed from contests for pro-Obama user-generated designs – the history of the politicization of design is also a history of disintermediation, and therefore of deprofessionalization. But it is also one of hyper-professionalization, as new figures emerge in the wake of new tools and channels, from social media managers to data scientists (AI-oriented spin doctors, when?). Thus, disintermediation is always ambiguous. Biasetton tackles this dramatic mutation of the political media landscape without moralism. Her approach is analytically useful, since some of the slogans of the Atelier Populaire – never not historically eulogized – such as "*toute la presse est toxique*", could well be adopted (and perhaps have been) by flat-Earthers and other conspiratorial movements.

The inspiration for this book's title comes from Dante, who likened the political condition of his time to "a ship without a pilot in great tempest". Designers like to think of themselves as the pilot, but it's time to accept that this ship is unmanned: as Biasetton puts it, "it is almost impossible for designers to be 'in control' of anything, least of all production means". The means of production in communication design – that is, media – affect one another in surprising, non-teleological ways. For instance, in the following pages we find out how the hegemony of television propelled a poster renaissance. However, with the rise of the "metamedium" (the computer), the real paradigmatic shift is from media to *content*. This is rather bad news for designers, since they are traditionally media-oriented, whereas content, this ineffable entity, is media-agnostic. These are some of the reasons why, as Biasetton points out, the idea of a guidebook for political communication, although appealing, would be disingenuous.

Looking at both famous and little-known case studies from France, the US, the UK and Italy, *Superstorm* offers a practical model to frame the relationships between design and politics: design *with* politics, design *about* politics and design *of* politics. While the first relationship is established and the second is somehow safe, the last one is certainly the most challenging, thus, the most intriguing. Design *of* politics is the way ahead to avoid "design autarchy" (which is not the same as design autonomy). Sure, there's no guidebook for that, but Biasetton doesn't shy away from providing some guidelines. She urges us to realize that design + politics does not always = activism, that new struggles require new weapons, but also that "political interventions become real opportunities in light of specific and fortunate circumstances". In other words, communication designers must not confuse cause and effect: they shouldn't praise the visual means of a campaign only because it turned out to be politically successful or, reversely, mock it only because it led to political failure.

Silvio Lorusso
September 2023

INTRODUCTION

Throughout history, politics and images have always been intertwined, affecting profoundly citizens' interpretation of power and democracy. This is all the more true in the current screen-saturated Western culture, where users absorb more information through visual means than at any point in history. As a matter of fact, if one observes the leading role played by images on a political level in the last sixty years, it seems clear that Western societies have entered a stage that is increasingly dominated by the hegemony of the visual sphere. Evolving from propagandistic and televised communication frameworks typical of traditional media, today's Western political visual culture is becoming increasingly ubiquitous, faster, and accessible. In particular, within the last fifteen years, the advent of social networking sites has caused traditional forms of political campaigning such as posters, flyers, and rallies to progressively move online and assume new, different and unexpected forms. And, due to their capacity for interactivity, it is now possible to witness an increasingly complex, multifaceted, and networked system of political images and their meaning-making process – which often encompasses unforeseeable interactions with online users.

On the one hand, the deployment of social networking sites for political campaigning and candidates' self-promotion demonstrates a continuity of the centrality of the political visual image pursued throughout the 20th century. On the other hand, however, the introduction of new forms of communication within Western politics displays major changes in the potentialities for interactivity which, even in the most rudimentary way, capture forms of participatory culture and yet unimagined systems of user engagement. Indeed, as new media technologies allow greater access to media authoring and editing tools, Western democracies see a multitude of actors – from spin doctors to online users – contributing to the creation of today's political visual culture. Moreover, the internet and especially social networking sites impose certain constraints, afford certain actions, and reward certain behaviors – thus becoming fundamental means involved in any image-making process. And whilst data mining models allow politicians to predict the voting behavior of citizens and the online users mobilize through the use of social networking sites, communication designers are increasingly questioning their agency within this rapidly changing landscape.

As contemporary politics relies heavily on new media technologies for their communication, from online voting systems to Instagram posts, communicative artifacts and design processes are increasingly involved in the visual outcome of politics. However, at a time when communication designers are striving to bring their voice to issues that matter, they have to face a visual culture able to sway political perception as well as new systems of image-making which often seem to limit their agency, or at least drastically put it into question.

In this complex and multifaceted context, designers appear to be facing a stalemate in their ability to act, leading to a noticeable retreat from meaningful engagement with the social sphere. This setback has become particularly apparent as society confronts the recent upheavals shaping the Western political landscape.

Let's consider, for example, the campaign for Britain's Brexit vote in 2015, where an impressive amount of disguised social pressures and suppressed rage found expression through new forms of political communication, both on the side of political actors and citizens themselves. While the Remain and Leave factions were campaigning, facts displayed on polished posters claiming that 'the EU has brought peace to 28 member states' or that 'in Poland or Hungary the EU is seen as the last defense against their authoritarian governments' were apparently not as convincing as the powerful and concise promise of Leave's 'Take back control' printed on double-decker buses (FIG. 1, 2). In the year where 'post-truth' was proclaimed international word of the year by the Oxford Dictionary, Trump's election as the 45th president of the U.S. showed how most of a campaign's image assets could be customized from voter to voter by adopting data analysis techniques based on the psychological insights of large numbers of people – a fact that no carefully designed newsletter could have or will ever surmount.

In the following U.S. presidential campaign, billionaire and democratic candidate Michael Bloomberg was advised by his campaign manager to hire some of the most popular accounts on Instagram to craft custom satirical memes that could make him more relatable to social media users (FIG. 3), showcasing the relevance (albeit marginally) of online vernacular design within political communication systems.

In 2020, as the COVID-19 pandemic unfolded, politicians made extensive use of their mediatized presence in order to appease, agitate or explain complex situations to their citizens, perpetuating forms of populist communication which designers seem unwilling to confront – or at least acknowledge. And in 2022, millions of short videos were uploaded on TikTok by Ukrainian and Russian combat soldiers with the hashtag #foryoupage, contributing to a distorted (and often disturbing) perception of the invasion of Russia in the Ukrainian territory, which will likely have a greater resonance to a significant portion of the worldwide audience if compared to any other visual information provided by traditional mainstream media.

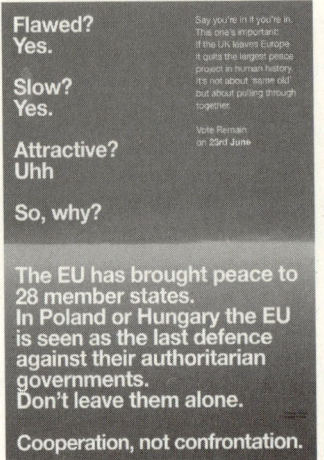

FIG. 1–2
Wolfgang Tillmans / Between Bridges, Pro-EU / Anti-Brexit campaign.
Mar – Jun 2016. Source: tillmans.co.uk. Copyright: Wolfgang Tillmans.

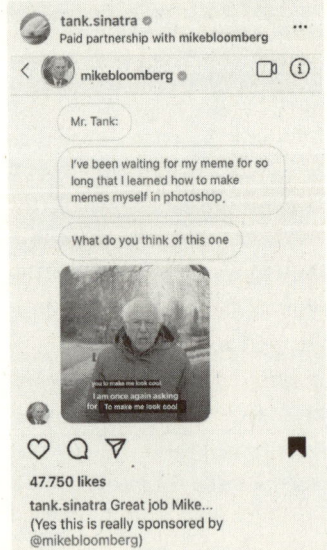

FIG. 3
Screenshot from the IG page
@tank.sinatra, 13 Feb 2020.
Source: Instagram.
Copyright: Tank Sinatra.

One of the main issues at the heart of this book is that the role of communication design within the processes that make up the visual culture of Western politics has been rarely problematized, especially within the last fifteen years. This does not mean, of course, that the relationship between design practice and forms of political representation has not been addressed in recent times. Indeed, books like *Iron Fists* (2008) by Steven Heller, *Graphic Agitation* (2006) and *Visual Impact* (2015) by Liz McQuiston, *Design and Political Dissent* (2020) by Jilly Traganou or even catalogs such as *Branding Terror* (2013) by Artur Beifuss & Francesco Trivini Bellini have provided scholars and practitioners – myself included – with fundamental knowledge and references for orienting ourselves in the complex relationship between design, media and politics.

However, these researchers often present similar starting points and modalities of investigation. In the cases of Heller and Beifuss & Trivini Bellini, for example, the authors report on historical or contemporary constructions of communication systems in specific circumstances (i.e. 20th-century totalitarian regimes or terrorist groups) by comparing them to modern corporate and branding strategies. The works of McQuiston and Traganou, instead, investigate the practice of design as a vehicle for social change solely or mostly through the lens of grassroots activism.

Overall, these studies produce informed archives of visual artifacts during times of turmoil, but often seem to create a schism between 'evil' communication and 'good' communication – the first one in reference to well-thought out branding systems managed by vicious totalitarian and terrorist groups, and the second one in reference to creatively expressed social and political acts of dissent. Furthermore, it often appears that the role of new media technologies is only loosely taken into account when assessing the impact that design can have within the field of political communication.

These aspects have prompted me to investigate a number of key issues. For example, whether the paradigm of 'design + politics = activism' is preventing the emergence of new modes of intervention by designers in the Western political scene. But also, why digital artifacts within this field are frequently omitted or understudied in favor of paper or 'analog' ones such as posters, prints, murals, and ballots. And lastly, if it is possible to expand the investigation of designers and the practice of design itself within the field of political communication beyond the analysis of communication artifacts and into a larger and more interdisciplinary field of study.

Based on these questions, this book is founded on the hypothesis that communication design has been struggling to find a new agency in the Western political landscape of the last fifteen years, causing a stalemate that prevents design from interacting with it. The second hypothesis is that this stalemate may be caused by a clash between the discourse of design and the vortex of perpetual and unforeseeable processes of social transformation caused by the intermingling of new media technologies and political communication – a powerful ensemble which we will refer to from now on as the Superstorm.

NOTES ON THE SUPERSTORM

Although the word 'superstorm' refers to a specific meteorological situation, it has never been officially recognized by the World Meteorological Organization, nor by any other scientific institution around the world. In fact, Andrew (1992), Katrina (2005), Sandy (2012) and Harvey (2017) have all been identified as hurricanes and further distinguished according to their specific characteristics (such as 'tropical cyclone', 'extra-tropical cyclone', or 'post-tropical cyclone'). Nevertheless, the term arose spontaneously in reference to the 1993 nor'easter that raged from Florida to New England in March of that year, when both citizens and the press were in search of a word that could express the disaster that stood before them. Also dubbed 'the Storm of the Century' or 'the Great Blizzard', the storm of 1993 was characterized by unprecedented coastal flooding, high winds, rain and record snowfall. Since then, the term 'superstorm' has been commonly used in the U.S. as a reference to unusual and unforeseen hurricanes which hit the land with a destructive and disruptive force. At the same time, in literature, the words 'storm' or 'tempest' have often been used as powerful metaphors to define a catastrophic and frightful series of events which determined, or were the cause of, a specific situation.

This is for example the case of Dante, who in the second half of the sixth canto of Purgatory makes use of an apostrophe to express his anxiety towards the political conditions of 14th-century's Italy, which he defines as "a ship without a pilot in great tempest" (canto VI, vv. 76-78). Three centuries later, in Shakespeare's *The Tempest* (1611), readers are once again invited into a world that seems far removed from our own, but is rife with familiar concerns about freedom, power, and control. Through the stories of Prospero, Miranda, Ariel, Caliban, Antonio and all the other characters, the author shows us the intricate dynamics of rival factions in hot pursuit of power – be it over the land, other people, or their own destiny. Shakespeare knows that power is always a moving subject, and as he reveals the characters' dark histories and strips society down to its basest desires, he invites the reader to wonder if this vicious cycle will ever end. In both Dante's and Shakespeare's works, the tempest represents a disturbance of the social order, an image of chaos, and the uncertainty and ruthlessness of political power. But the metaphor of the tempest is not just limited to this. In the ninth chapter of Golding's *Lord of the Flies* (1954), for example, a violent storm batters the island immediately after the group of surviving boys murders one of their own. In the midst of the whipping rain, the murder of Simon pounds home the catastrophe of unleashed barbarism and embodies the chaos and anarchy that have overtaken the island, foreshadowing further acts of violence to come. Golding uses the storm to symbolize a drastic and tragic change – that the once innocent boys have lost their humanity, and that the island has become a place of irrevocable mayhem. The storm is, in Golding's view, a point of no return which marks an indelible border between the before and the after, upsetting the known order forever.

In this book, I will use the term Superstorm as a conceptual and narrative metaphor to illustrate the evolution of the relationship between political communication and new media technologies, which since the 1960s has begun to intertwine and give life to the Western political visual culture as it is known today. As much as the hurricanes that hit the north-eastern lands of the United States and the rhetorical devices of the storm in the works of Dante, Shakespeare and Golding, the Superstorm represents a cyclone of unforeseen magnitude which is slowly but steadily engulfing the Western social sphere.

However, unlike the actual storms and the rhetorical figures narrated by the aforementioned authors, this one never seems to subside. The Superstorm, indeed, consists of communication processes which are constantly evolving but that nonetheless can be subsumed within the same motive power. Within the Superstorm, communication design plays a pivotal role because it represents the projectual act that is inherent and gives life to new communication processes.

Therefore, in order to understand the role of communication design and communication designers within the Superstorm, one must remember that this cyclone involves elements, relationships and contexts of the present and of the past, all of which are in constant flux.

ON READING THE SUPERSTORM

The book is structured as a cross-disciplinary historical and critical study that outlines the relationship between design, political communication and new media technologies between the 1960s and 2020 from the point of view of design culture and through the narrative metaphor of the Superstorm. In the context of this study, the term 'design culture' harks back to Guy Julier's seminal text *The Culture of Design* (2013), in which the British design professor explains how this term can be employed as an academic discipline that engages with the social sciences – as well as an object of study and a form of critical practice that faces contemporary social and political challenges. To investigate the concept of design culture, Julier starts from the assumption that "culture is no longer one of pure representation or narrative where the visual conveys messages", and argues that design should no longer be conceived as "the creation of visual artifacts to be used or 'read'", but rather as "the structuring of systems of encounter within the visual and material world"[1].

Julier's point is that the meaning, function and value of design artifacts depend on a complex patchwork of other variables, which he identifies as "the triangulation of the activities of designers, production and consumption"[2] (FIG. 4). The adoption of multiple points of view within the analysis of design artifacts is based on the conviction that design culture, as noted by Julier, "is part of the flows of global culture. It is located within network society and is also an instrument of it"[3]. Therefore, the interpretation of one or more design artifacts within a concept of design culture

---

[1] G. JULIER, *The Culture of Design* (Los Angeles: SAGE, 2013), 11.
[2] IBID, 14.
[3] IBID, 6.

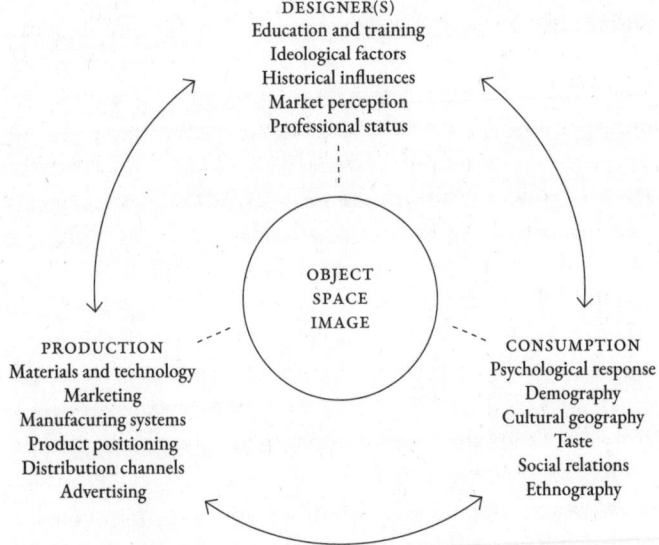

FIG. 4
Domains of design culture. Elaboration from Julier's figure (2013, p. 15).

> "requires one to both undertake close analysis of that object while also keeping another eye on its relationship to other visual, spatial and material expressions that contribute to the constitution of its meaning"[4].

This is particularly true when dealing with visual artifacts and communication design which, as noted by Australian design professor Veronika Kelly, "both shapes and is shaped by social conditions and culture that has recourse to the positions made available and those taken up in a discourse"[5].

[4] IBID, 14.
[5] V. KELLY, "Culture, Practice, Discourse: A Theoretical Framework for a Critical Approach to Communication Design," *Studies in Material Thinking* 15, NO. 4 (2016): 12.

Since the aim of this book is to investigate the current status of the relationship between political communication and the design discourse within the Western political landscape, the research is not focused on communication design artifacts *per se*, but rather on how communication designers respond to the intertwining of political communication and new media technologies from the 1960s to the present day – hence the Superstorm.

Within this book, design discourse refers to the sum of "text, talk, and constructive actions" that are "consensually maintained and advanced by members of communities who identify themselves in terms of its premises, practices, and resulting artifacts"[6] within the Western communication design scenario (even though, as will be further specified in the section *Research Considerations*, the term 'Western' is subject to several biases). As such, the book will employ a variety of texts of different nature, whose quantity and variety will change radically from one chapter to the other due to the non-linearity of the research.

At the same time, the book will analyze a series of communication design artifacts which are not produced by designers recognized as such. Indeed, the word 'designer' will be used to identify anyone who adopts the means of production, consumption and distribution within the creation of the Western visual political culture. This use of the terms 'design' and 'designer' in their wider, most intelligible meaning is at no point meant to be provocative, but neither is it neutral. As I will explain in detail in the chapter *Design and the Superstorm*, this choice represents an opportunity to reflect on the consequences of the ever-increasing ubiquity and reach of political communication due to the advances of new media technology. In this sense, this 'expanded view' on design artifacts may be

---

[6] K. KRIPPENDORFF, "Design Discourse," in *Design Discourse* (Bielefeld: transcript Verlag, 2021), 336.

able to reflect a multifaceted context in which both designers and users contribute to the shaping of culture and reality, shifting design research "from linear flows of meaning to complex, multi-linear ecologies that involve ongoing interactions between design and its human and other participants"[7]. According to German communication scholar Klaus Krippendorff, this shift in the understanding design culture represents an utter "epistemological challenge" which "lies in abandoning the naïve conception of an objective and universally shared reality in which their design enters, is used as intended and by everyone alike", which often "leaves no space for non-designers to see their world differently without being judged wrong"[8]. Contrarily, the study and careful observation of design artifacts within a larger and interdisciplinary framework might be helpful to detangle the complex weave of meanings and usages that a design artifact naturally welcomes.

Another important insight provided by Julier is that "a Design Culture enquiry traces a cartography that exposes and analyzes the linkages of artifacts that constitute information flows and the spaces between them", both by analyzing individual artifacts "relationally to other artifacts, processes and systems" and by engendering "a generative mode that produces new sensibilities, attitudes, approaches and intellectual processes within design"[9]. To achieve this, writes Julier, "Design Culture [...] moves across traditional design disciplines, plunders other academic traditions (particularly in the humanities and social sciences) and is promiscuous in its coupling with their related theoretical perspectives"[10].

[7] G. JULIER AND A. V. MUNCH, "Introducing Design Culture," in *Design Culture: Objects and Approaches*, ed. Guy Julier et al. (London: Bloomsbury Publishing, 2019), 3.

[8] KRIPPENDORFF, "Design Discourse," 339.

[9] JULIER, *The Culture of Design*, 16.

[10] IBID, 18.

Following Julier's considerations, the present book is built upon a non-linear narrative of events which aims at building a non-exhaustive critical genealogy of the relationship between political communication, new media technologies and communication design from the 1960s to 2020 and across Western countries. The genealogy's non-linearity is dictated by a selection of historical periods which focuses on three key events in the history of new media technologies, and which will serve as reference points to outline the evolution (or birth) of debates and practices concerning the culture of design within the evolution of the Superstorm. To formulate this genealogy, the book merges different fields of knowledge – mainly related to political theory, sociology, media studies and cultural studies – which will hopefully contribute to a more all-encompassing perspective on the reasons behind this stalemate.

The (non-exhaustive) selection of salient moments in history related to the evolution of media technology also draws inspiration from the works of numerous scholars in the field of sociology and media studies who have long been wondering about the complex interrelation between the development of Western societies and media technology.

These works refer in particular to the studies conducted by a series of intellectuals and academics who, starting from the 1950s, have adopted a specific method of inquiry which analyzes how the introduction of a specific medium or set of media influenced how individuals and societies think and behave in a given time span. Works such as *Empire and Communications* (1950) by Canadian professor Harold Innis, *The Gutenberg Galaxy: The Making of Typographic Man* (1962) by Canadian philosopher and media theorist Marshall McLuhan, and *Orality and Literacy* (1982) by American professor Walter Ong and are all examples of this analytical structure, which is mostly based on a critical re-evaluation of the role of media within history – albeit with very different academic and stylistic approaches.

The structure of the present book is inspired in particular by the trilogy *The Information Age: Economy, Society and Culture* by Spanish sociologist Manuel Castells – composed of *The Rise of the Network Society* (1996), *The Power of Identity* (1997), and *End of Millennium* (1998) – which depicts the emergence of a new society dictated by the structural transformations in the relationships of production, power, and experience after the introduction of new media technologies.

The work of Castells is fundamental for this book due to his spatial and (especially) temporal re-ordering of the Information Age, which according to the author,

> "originated in the historical coincidence, around the late 1960s and mid-1970s, of three independent processes: the information technology revolution; the economic crisis of both capitalism and statism, and their subsequent restructuring; and the blooming of cultural social movements, such as libertarianism, human rights, feminism, and environmentalism"[11].

And it is precisely the interaction between these processes which, according to Castells, led to a "substantial modification of social forms of space and time, and to the emergence of a new culture"[12].

Inspired by Castells' temporal patterning of the Information Age, the present book will develop through three main historical periods, which feature the early formulations of computer-mediated communications in the mid-1960s and early 1970s, the diffusion of the internet and personal computers between the late 1980s and early 1990s, and the spread

---

[11] M. CASTELLS, *End of Millennium* (Blackwell Publishers, 1998), 372.
[12] IBID, 376.

of social networking sites starting from the early 2000s. The selected periods, however, are not solely defined by technological changes and do not intend to pursue a technologically deterministic view of history, for it is not the aim of this book to gain a better or new understanding of the functioning of political communication according to the evolution of new media technologies. Instead, the selection of the historical periods will be used as a guide to build a non-exhaustive genealogy, based on the narrative metaphor of the Superstorm, aimed at investigating the reasons that brought the discourse of design to a stalemate with relation to political communication.

BOOK STRUCTURE

This book is structured in three chapters which diachronically explore the evolution of the Superstorm and its interaction with the field of communication design. The first chapter, *Genealogy of the Superstorm*, offers a synthetic overview of the changes that occurred in political communication and communication design concurrently with the emergence of new media. In particular, the chapter looks at the 1960s and early 1970s as a meeting ground where new social, political, and technological circumstances shed a fresh light on the relationship between politics, media, and images, giving life to the Superstorm. To this end, this chapter investigates how the fields of political communication, new media, and communication design began to interact with one another in the Western societies of the 1960s by tackling each of them in a specific section.

In the second chapter, *Anatomy of the Superstorm*, the concept of mediatization will be used as a starting point to decipher the effects of the collision between new media logic(s) and the field of political communication, which increased the visibility of the Superstorm as well as its complexity. The sections in this chapter analyze how the internet has had an impact on the systems of production, distribution, and reception of political imagery, causing great alterations both in the Western political discourse and in the role of designers willing to take part in it. More specifically, this chapter offers a confrontation between the issues of agency, mediation, and authorship in light of the processes of spectacularization, disintermediation, and personalization to be read through the lens of mediatization. To provide a meaningful picture of how these three processes and issues shape today's political visual culture, they will be paired with each other in order to investigate their problematic nature as well as their diachronic and propositive ones.

Lastly, the third chapter, *Design and the Superstorm*, investigates three different ways in which communication design has been employed within the Superstorm during the last fifteen years. In this context, political visual culture comprises the totality of the images that make up the Western political context, together with the technologies with which those images are produced, elaborated, and distributed, the uses to which they are subjected, and the social effects they elicit.

The analysis makes use of three categories in which the selected case studies are placed. Specifically, design *with* politics describes the collaboration between a designer or design firm and a politician or political party; design *about* politics refers to the use of conceptual and operative design tools for researching and exposing political issues; and design *of* politics indicates designerly ways of conceiving, creating and managing political communication without the declared presence of any designer recognized as such.

Overall, the aim of this book is to provide a record of the transformations caused by the Superstorm and its intensification, and eventually to determine if, and in what ways, it is possible to outline a scope of action for communication designers within this complex and ever-growing force.

RESEARCH CONSIDERATIONS

The book in its entirety should be considered in the light of some considerations, which are helpful to delineate the perimeter of this study as well as its future directions. The first one can be found within the structuring and recomposition of the historical background of the research. In fact, although the research questions are entirely rooted in the analysis of design discourse, the book draws from a heterogeneous compound of different fields of knowledge – mainly from the social sciences – in order to compose its analytical framework.

On the one hand, this aspect has managed to provide a somewhat comprehensive picture of the Superstorm, obtained through the account of different historical periods which placed the design discourse within a multilateral perspective. On the other hand, however, this broad-reaching view might have resulted in a skewed or unbalanced characterization of the authors and theories cited.

Design culture as a mode of inquiry is historically constituted and formed through its relations to other disciplines due to its unfolding, contingent and dynamic nature[13]. Therefore, for the purpose of this study, I deemed it necessary to explore disciplinary territories contiguous to mine, with the purpose of reading them through the lenses of design culture and in order to provide a different gaze on a relationship (that of communication design and political communication) which has been mostly studied solely through design artifacts alone.

The second consideration, instead, concerns my stance towards the researched topics, which is, inevitably, not neutral. In particular, although the book seeks to offer a narrative – that of the Superstorm – which it is said to encompass most Western countries, the research only addresses case studies of

---

[13] See JULIER AND MUNCH, *Design Culture*, 5–6.

(almost) only Italian and North American political scenarios. On the one hand, this stance is based on the fact that this study addresses the visual aspects of political communication, which require a proper understanding of the vernacular forms of image production and circulation, such as cross-references to elements of popular culture, inside jokes that are developed within specific online niches, as well as allusions to past political experiences which are now part of the collective memory of a specific country. On the other hand, I recognize that the lack of case studies coming from other Western countries might weaken the book, which would rather benefit from a more expanded perspective in order to justify what is deemed to be a 'Western' phenomenon.

These shortcomings, however, can represent a challenge for the present research, whose overarching and possibly overambitious scope could turn into a collaborative quest to explore the effects that the Superstorm has and will have on the design discourse from a variety of social, political and cultural viewpoints.

I
GENEALOGY OF THE SUPERSTORM.
NEW MEDIA, POLITICS, AND DESIGN

Between the 1960s and early 1970s, the Western world reshaped itself through a series of technological and social changes which have helped make it as it is known today. In those years, the U.S. and many European countries witnessed a slew of initiatives aimed at altering the status quo and shifting societal norms from the bottom to the top. Dissatisfied with the current state of affairs, a record number of young people began to question society's patriarchal, extractive, militarist, and racist decisions, with the goal of providing solutions for peaceful and collaborative coexistence on Earth.

In the meantime, the use of microelectronics in the aerospace industry urged a leap forward in the development of electronic circuits, reducing not only their mass but also production costs. The miniaturization of components and the ability to implement extremely complex functions on the basis of binary logic (comprised of the elementary states 0 and 1) allowed for the representation and elaboration of signals using digital (or numerical) technology, which consists in the acquisition, transmission, and transformation of binary sequences, as well as the execution of various mathematical operations.

The coincidence of these two simultaneous elements – apparently distant from each other – is actually at the heart of the emergence of the so-called 'new media' as it is often referred to nowadays. In fact, at a time when the availability of reliable and low-cost circuits made it possible to build the first personal computers (allowing further developments in the fields of human-machine interfaces, operating systems, and algorithm development), many of the issues raised by counter-cultural movements started being addressed by students and researchers who began to speculate on the use of the computer beyond military purposes and imagined a world characterized by the circulation of free information.

After a great leap forward in microelectronics, a multitude of diverse actors in the U.S. took part in a wide debate on the features and objectives of personal computers and networks – laying the foundations of our contemporary understanding of the term 'new media'. During years of absolute television predominance, the introduction of new media into the media matrix of the 1960s also sparked great interest among various academic fields, which turned into an opportunity to revisit the role of images in the functioning of political communication. In particular, the emergence of new media brought to light new features and potentialities regarding the fruition of *all* media, together with a broad reflection on their application in social and political contexts.

Clearly, in the 1960s, the fact that images were important carriers of political information was nothing new *per se*. On the contrary, the previous decades had demonstrated the centrality of the image in the construction of 20th-century totalitarian leaders worldwide. Studies such as *Iron Fists* (2008) by Steven Heller, for example, show in detail how visual elements were part of sophisticated strategies aimed at selling the totalitarian message, and altogether highlight the high degree of awareness involved in their manufacturing process. However, a series of technological, social, and cultural changes starting from the 1960s laid the foundations for a redefinition of *what* an image is in terms of political communication. In this context of great political, social and technological change, communication design in the Western world began to acquire new roles in the interaction with the socio-political sphere. Both in the U.S. and

Europe, communication designers started to experiment with new ways to voice or reflect on social claims and political issues, which ended up reviewing their very role and agency as well as the spaces and places of their practice.

The 1960s and early 1970s represent a unique window of time as it saw the extraordinary convergence of different contexts of reflection and application at a time of great technological advancement. The cultural climate formed between these years is critical for this study because it is exactly at this time that it is possible to trace the origins of the relationship between communication design, political communication and new media – three fields which gave life to a long-lasting yet quite tumultuous interplay in the years to come.

LIGHTS, CAMERA, ACTION

In a scenario marked by threats of escalating warfare, political instability, and heightened global competition, two candidates with very different views on the future of the U.S. ran in the 44th quadrennial presidential election: John Fitzgerald Kennedy and Richard Nixon. The young Massachusetts senator and Eisenhower's sitting vice president campaigned tirelessly in the summer of 1960 through political rallies and national conventions but, with Nixon slightly ahead in the polls by the end of the summer, Kennedy decided to challenge him to a series of televised debates in the upcoming month. And so, on 26 September 1960, at the CBS broadcast facility in downtown Chicago, the two running candidates competed in the first nationally televised presidential debate in American history – the first in a long series to follow.

From that day on, the debate gave rise to a surfeit of myths and continues to be the subject of several conflicting interpretations. One prevailing myth is especially related to the alleged effects of the debate on two different audiences, with the belief that those who *listened* to the debate on the radio pronounced Nixon the winning candidate while those who *watched* the debate on TV thought Kennedy was undisputedly the triumphant one.

The debate went down in history not only for the fate of the upcoming elections but also (and mostly) for the discussion it elicited on the relationship between media, images, and politics. It was at this time, in fact, that many emerging critics and scholars from different academic backgrounds began to point at media to understand their "effects" on politics. Among others, media theorist Marshall McLuhan devoted a fair number of pages to the debate in his seminal 1964 book *Understanding Media*, arguing confidently that "Without TV, Nixon had it made"[14]. Aside from the determinism that pervades them, such convictions raise interesting questions about *what* made the Kennedy-Nixon debate such a momentous event, and *why* precisely at that time in history.

According to history, Kennedy and Nixon had been preparing very differently for the evening of the debate. Specifically, whilst the first would be remembered for the careful preparation of his appearance on the small screen, the second was unfortunately physically incapacitated and gave the impression of being "unaware" of the impact that this event could have on the American public. The story goes that Kennedy spent the weekend before the debate in a hotel with his speechwriter and political advisor Ted Sorensen assessing possible questions in the debate, and devoted much attention to the *construction* of his image on television. He met the day before the debate with the producer to discuss the design of the set and the placement of the cameras, wore a blue suit to minimize the glare of the camera lights and create contrast with the gray background of the studio, and put on a little makeup too.

---

[14] M. MCLUHAN, *Understanding Media: The Extensions of Man* (New York: McGraw-Hill, 1964), 330.

In contrast, Nixon was still recovering from a painful knee injury that occurred during a campaign trail in North Carolina which caused him to appear sallow and underweight. This accident also caused him to miss the opportunity of looking at the stage or knowing the position of the cameras in advance, which ultimately resulted in a vacant look throughout the whole debate. Lastly, unlike his opponent, Nixon opted for no makeup and wore a gray suit – which made him look drained and blended into the television set. Although much of the choices undertaken by Kennedy may seem trivial, they are very important because they underline a meticulous care towards the *production* of the televised image.

At this point, it should be noted that Kennedy was not the first one to use the medium of television during a political campaign. On the contrary, in 1952 Eisenhower pioneered the idea of a television-based campaign strategy with his renowned series of ads *Eisenhower Answers America* (FIG. 5). The ads were produced by Rosser Reeves, a widely renowned adman from the 1950s and member of the Ted Bates advertising agency, who advised Eisenhower that the campaign should run brief commercials. The result was a series of twenty-second ads featuring 'everyday' Americans asking Eisenhower questions about day-to-day issues such as inflation, taxes, living costs, the war in Korea and more (FIG. 6).

Overall, the implementation of political ads on television showed many new features that this medium could afford. In particular, that the citizens used in the ads could reflect a broad spectrum of voters (not only based on their physical appearance but also on their dialect), and that the airing of the ads could be accurately targeted, both in counties and states. Altogether, these characteristics allowed the *Eisenhower Answers America* ads to be innovative in the way political communication was produced, distributed and consumed – but did not differ from the kind of advertising to which Americans were accustomed back in the 1950s. In fact, the ads produced by Reeves for Eisenhower made use of actual selling lines based on a left-right rhythm of dialogue, and strongly resembled the TV ads he produced at Ted Bates for the sale of commercial products.

FIG. 5
Still image of the introduction to the ad series *Eisenhower answers America* (1952). Copyright: Dwight D. Eisenhower Presidential Library. Source: Museum of the Moving Image, livingroomcandidate.org

FIG. 6
Stills from the ads *Eisenhower answers America* (1952). Copyright: Dwight D. Eisenhower Presidential Library. Source: Museum of the Moving Image, livingroomcandidate.org

For this reason, we could say that Eisenhower and Kennedy made two very different uses of the television medium: if Eisenhower was the first politician to employ an advertising agency to produce TV ads to set out his political agenda, Kennedy would later realize that TV could enable him to promote (or amplify) his *own* self-image. This difference represents a turning point in the attitude towards the visual aspects of political representation and underlines an important passage in the history of political communication, for Kennedy harnessed the television medium by understanding new features of its *cultural functioning*.

To better understand this point, one needs to consider the Kennedy-Nixon debate not as an isolated episode but rather as the culmination of a slow and steady process carried out by Kennedy, in which the construction of his image took place. Long before his candidacy for president, in fact, Kennedy had already developed a considerably alluring image both as a military hero through his Navy service during World War II, and as a man of letters with the publication of two books and the receipt of a Pulitzer Prize. At the same time, after his 1952 Senate victory and his marriage to Jacqueline Bouvier the following year, he began to be seen as a political star in the making and a symbol of the modern family man.

From 1953 onwards, magazines such as LIFE and Time began to show interest not just in Kennedy's political life (FIG. 8, 10), but also in his personal one – with covers portraying him with his wife during leisure time (FIG. 7), with his family (FIG. 9, 12), or even picturing his wife in the foreground (FIG. 11). And as coverage of him in the press became correspondingly vast, his image sparked great grassroots excitement in the U.S. and triggered great expectations for his political future in Western democracies. But magazines were not the only media interested in this rising political star. On the contrary, Kennedy developed an all-encompassing communication strategy which contributed to an overall sympathetic media coverage. For example, he was the first politician of some note to appear in an evening show, and specifically as guest of Jack Paar at *The Tonight Show* during the race for the democratic nomination in 1959. Furthermore, iconic personalities such as Frank Sinatra and Harry Belafonte stood publicly beside Kennedy – the first one by providing him with a revisited version of his classic song *High Hopes* (which eventually became the theme of JFK's election campaign), and the second one by appearing in one of his many TV ads.

Lastly, filmmaker Robert Drew was given intimate access to Kennedy to produce a documentary, which eventually gave rise

FIG. 7
LIFE Magazine, Vol. 35 NO. 3 (July 1953). Cover by Hy Peskin. Copyright: LIFE. Source: books.google.it

FIG. 8
Time Magazine, Vol. LXX NO. 23 (December 1957). Cover by Henry Koerner. Copyright: Time USA, LLC. Source: content.time.com

FIG. 9
LIFE Magazine, Vol. 44 NO. 16 (April 1958). Cover by Nina Leen. Copyright: LIFE. Source: books.google.it

FIG. 10
Time Magazine, Vol. LXXII NO. 21 (November 1958). Cover by Boris Chaliapin. Copyright: Time USA, LLC. Source: content.time.com

FIG. 11
LIFE Magazine, Vol. 47 NO. 8 (August 1959). Cover by Mark Shaw. Copyright: LIFE. Source: books.google.it

FIG. 12
Time Magazine Vol. LXXVI NO. 2 (July 1960). Cover by Bernard Safran. Copyright: Time USA, LLC. Source: content.time.com

to images of remarkable intimacy. Drew's work eventually resulted in three films – *Primary* (1960), *Adventures on the New Frontier* (1961), and *Crisis* (1963) – and one short movie released after the president's assassination called *Faces of November* (1964). Although the films did not initially succeed in any network broadcasting, they proved to be of great relevance to film history as pillars of 'cinéma vérité', a distinctive approach to documentary filmmaking developed in the early 1960s that focused on the spontaneous activities of subjects through the camera. Drew recorded events as they were happening, without direction, allowing characters to move in a real-life story in front of the camera lens, and thus revolutionized the art of editing by cutting on "picture logic" as opposed to "word logic"[15].

Within the context of this chapter, the Kennedy-Nixon debate should not be understood as a nostalgic sojourn, but rather as a starting point for a broader reflection on the surrounding social, political and technological circumstances that surrounded the event – which was a pivotal moment for the field of political communication. As American Professor of Electronic Media Mary Ann Watson underlines, "The presidential election of 1960 was to be a barometer of a new era. It represented a shift in American political technique and underscored the forcefulness of television in the formation of public opinion"[16]. But also, Kennedy's use of the media suggested a new and larger trajectory that political communication was moving on in the 1960s – which unfolded gradually as new kinds of media began to shape new logics of image production, distribution, and consumption.

This 'new era' inaugurated the development of a new political image on the Western political scene, laying the foundations for a long-lasting legacy in the visual aspects of political

---

[15] S. MAMBER, *Cinema Verite in America: Studies In Uncontrolled Documentary* (Cambridge: MIT Press, 1974), 23.

[16] M. A. WATSON, *The Expanding Vista: American Television in the Kennedy Years* (Durham: Duke University Press, 1994), 4.

communication. Furthermore, these changing patterns in political communication paved the way for a series of reflections on the relationship between media, images, and politics which were still largely unaddressed in academia until the 1960s.

In fact, starting from those years, many scholars in the fields of communication and media studies demonstrated great interest in the role of images and media in political processes, whilst simultaneously raising great concerns about their effects on user-citizens. To a large extent, many remained suspicious about the relationship between images and politics, convinced that the aestheticization of politics caused by the media would lead to a degradation of rationality in the political realm and turn citizens into passive spectators.

Among them[17], most notably, we can find Max Horkheimer and Theodor W. Adorno, who coined the expression "culture industry" and considered media as instruments used to manipulate a passive audience in order to depoliticize the working class[18]. But also Jürgen Habermas, who in his seminal work *The Structural Transformation of the Public Sphere* highlighted how mass media in the 1960s operated in a vertical direction

---

[17] In light of what has been said so far, it should be noted that the thoughts of the authors cited below clearly do not take into account the complexity of their discourse nor the historical period in which they were elaborated. In this section of the study, the intent is to underline how a large portion of the academic thinking of the twenty-first century in the fields of philosophy and sociology on media has fueled a skewed perception over their role in society and on their effects on citizens. This is not the result of a lack of faith towards media by the cited authors, but rather the outcome of a conjunction of historical political and social events that eventually led to a general distrust of mediated imagery, especially if used for political purposes. This topic will be treated extensively in the introduction to the second chapter, Anatomy of the Superstorm.

[18] M. HORKHEIMER AND T. W. ADORNO, *Dialektik Der Aufklärung* (Amsterdam: Querido, 1947).

and with no interaction between producers and viewers, causing the medium to be simply consumed and thus annihilating the "public sphere", which according to the author constituted the basis of democratic debate and equality[19]. And finally Guy Debord, who through the conceptualization of the Spectacle raised a very severe critique of the role played by images (and especially television) in the lives of both individuals and the masses within capitalist societies[20] – and many more.

As scholars Giorgia Aiello and Katy Parry point out, this aversion toward the use of images in politics via electronic media is a recurrent theme in the 20th century, where the aestheticization of politics has often been connected with the fear of "turning citizens into passive spectators, entertained by the theatricalization of politics, but mystified as to how to participate as informed citizens"[21].

Nevertheless, despite their common mistrust of the role played by images on a social and political level, the research carried out from the 1960s onwards started attributing great importance to the visual aspects of political communication, and set the idea that the new logics of production, distribution, and consumption of political imagery enhanced by the evolution of media could generate new processes for the exercise of power and democracy.

---

[19] J. HABERMAS, *The Structural Transformation of the Public Sphere: An Inquiry Into a Category of Bourgeois Society* (Cambridge, MA: MIT Press, 1991).

[20] G. DEBORD, *The Society of the Spectacle* (Detroit: Black and Red, 1967).

[21] G. AIELLO AND K. PARRY, "Aesthetics, Political," in *The International Encyclopedia of Political Communication* (American Cancer Society, 2016), 3.

BAD MEDIA/GOOD MEDIA

In the introduction of this chapter, two questions were raised about the Kennedy-Nixon debate – namely *what* made the debate such a momentous event, and *why* precisely at that time in history. To the first question, I could suggest a twofold answer: on one hand, Kennedy highlighted a new direction for political communication characterized by a novel use of the media; on the other, as new kinds of media began to shape new logics of production, distribution, and consumption, many researchers started to devote their attention towards not only the content of political communication, but also its appearance. To the question of *why* this event has received such resonance precisely in those years, instead, we must open another section that deals with the emergence of new media.

One of the events that characterized the history of the U.S. in the 1960s was the launch of the Sputnik 1 satellite in 1957, which remained in orbit for almost three weeks before falling back into the atmosphere in January 1958. This event was of pivotal importance because, albeit at astronomical distances, the skies of the U.S. were breached, and for the first time Soviet supremacy in the field of space technology was openly manifested. The launch of the Sputnik 1 in particular made the U.S. realize the obsolescence of their projects in the field of technology applied to computers, and pushed the country towards new solutions to win back the space race. One of these was the establishment of a new research facility equipped with a substantial budget and able to promote other research centers: thus was born ARPA, acronym for Advanced Research Project Agency.

However, ARPA was not the only operational body employed to foster long-term advancement in the field of computer science. On the contrary, the 1960s and 1970s represent a unique timeframe as they saw the extraordinary convergence of different contexts of reflection and application at a time of great technological advancement. In fact, after a great leap forward in microelectronics, a multitude of diverse actors in the United States took part in a wide debate on the features and objectives of personal computers and networks. This discussion involved universities (e.g. UC Berkeley, UC Santa Barbara, Stanford University, Palo Alto Research Center, Honeywell) alongside intellectuals such as McLuhan, Illich, Nelson, Engelbart, Felsenstein, Brand, and many others. Together, these research centers and intellectuals explored hitherto unknown fields and moved towards an articulated research path that brought together utopias with cutting-edge projects, such as Sutherland's Sketchpad, Kay's DynaBook, ARPA's Arpanet, Xerox's Alto and many more.

The first years of ARPA were led by Joseph Licklider, a scientist and visionary who started pushing the culture of computer science towards a new direction that would eventually affect all future computer-related innovations[22]. Originally trained as an experimental psychologist, Licklider put his uniquely personal imprint on the research conducted at ARPA by bringing attention to topics like man-machine relationships and the idea of a computer-mediated communication[23].

In his vast academic production, there is one article called *The Computer as Communication Device*[24] which is of particular relevance to understand how computer science was developing in those years. In the article, written with Robert Taylor, the authors write:

---

[22] T. DETTI, "Joseph C. R. Licklider e le origini di Internet: tecnica, ricerca scientifica e società," *PC*, 2014, 167–7

[23] H. HENDERSON, *Communications and Broadcasting: From Wired Words to Wireless Web* (New York: Infobase Publishing, 2007), 124–29.

[24] J. C. R. LICKLIDER AND R. W. TAYLOR, "The Computer as a Communication Device," *Science and Technology*, 1968.

> "A communication engineer thinks of communicating as transferring information from one point to another in codes and signals. But to communicate is more than to send and to receive. [...] We believe that communicators have to do something nontrivial with the information they send and receive. And we believe that we are entering a technological age in which we will be able to interact with the richness of living information – not merely the passive way that we have become accustomed to [...] but as active participants in an ongoing process, bringing something to it through our interaction with it, and not simply receiving something from it by our connection to it"[25].

This passage is fundamental to understand the new vision that was beginning to form around new media, and that will influence the action of many communication designers both at that time in history as well as in future years. Specifically, we can start to observe the formation of the idea that 'old' media (such as television) could offer only a passive fruition, whereas the authors underline how new media envisage the development of a communitarian dimension – identified as a fundamental condition for the construction of a 'critical mass' and the diffusion of a network.

The idea of a collective network was widely debated in the early 1960s, and came as a direct influence of the countercultures that animate the political discourse of the U.S. in those years – which eventually shaped the first forms of cybercultures. Cybercultures were anti-authoritarian, close to pacifism, ecological movements, and the psychedelic revolution, and their aim was to disrupt the

---

[25] LICKLIDER & TAYLOR, "The Computer as a Communication Device". Quoted in Paul A. Mayer, *Computer Media and Communication: A Reader* (Oxford: Oxford University Press, 1999), 97.

(very firm) relationship between computer research, large-scale industry and the military apparatus. "To a generation that had grown up in a world beset by massive armies and by the threat of nuclear holocaust", as American Professor of Communication Fred Turner underlines, "the cybernetic notion of the globe as a single, interlinked pattern of information was deeply comforting: in the invisible play of information, many though they could see the possibility of global harmony"[26]. For young Americans embracing a cybernetic vision of the world, the main goal was to make technology more accessible and transform it from a "tool of oppression" to a "liberation tool".

This countercultural critique of hierarchical government and its celebration of cybernetic forms of collaborative organization was present in many projects which intended to show this alleged dichotomic purpose of technology. One of them is surely *Computer Lib/Dream Machines*[27], a volume written and self-published by American philosopher Ted Nelson in 1974 (FIG. 13) which opposed the idea of a joyful conviviality to the standardized and alienating industrial productivity.

Printed as a two-front-cover paperback, this large-sized volume (10.75 x 14 inches) consisted in a collage of typewritten fragments, hand-made cartoons, and black and white photocopies with the aim of "making people freer through computers"[28]. The cover of *Computer Lib* depicted a raised fist symbolizing the computer revolution as a cry of social protest, whilst the other side of the book, *Dream Machines*, showcased a young man wearing a superhero's cape who floats in a dark void and enters the light of a screen.

---

[26] F. TURNER, *From Counterculture to Cyberculture: Stewart Brand, the Whole Earth Network, and the Rise of Digital Utopianism* (Chicago: The University of Chicago Press, 2006), 5.
[27] T. H. NELSON, *Computer Lib: You Can and Must Understand Computers NOW / Dream Machines: New Freedoms Through Computer Screens — a Minority Report* (Chicago: Self-published, 1974).
[28] NELSON, *Computer Lib / Dream Machines*, DM 59.

In *Computer Lib*, Nelson illustrates both the technical and political aspects of computers, and envisions them as a means of education, whereas in *Dream Machines* he speculates on the future of the computers and their alternative uses. Drawing on Licklider's idea of a shared and collective network, Nelson thought that computers could enable active citizen participation and collaborative work processes for all users. Moreover, in *Computer Lib* Nelson preaches the liberation of the computer from the 'clutches' of big corporations like IBM (FIG. 14), which

FIG. 13
The two covers of Ted Nelson's *Computer Lib/Dream Machines* (1974).
Copyright: Mark Richards. Source: computerhistory.org

FIG. 14
Detail of page CL 52.

according to him embodied a form of centralized, expensive and bureaucratic informatics available only to military people, scientists and intellectuals. The work of Nelson is of pivotal importance to understand the divide between 'good' informatics and 'bad' informatics that emerged in the 1970s – which will result in a broader opposition between 'good' media and 'bad' media in the same years.

The countercultural and anti-hegemonic tone that pervades *Computer Lib/Dream Machines* is accompanied in the same years by a series of other projects that urged users to acquire a knowledge of computers and reject to think of them as mere scientific machines. Along the same lines, for example, was the bimonthly newsletter *People's Computer Company* (FIG. 15). Founded and produced by Bob Albrecht and George Firedrake in the early 1970s in Menlo Park, California, *PCC* took on the mission of extending access to technology and promote computer literacy. At a time when many computers were still kept solely in university rooms, *PCC* also served as an organization where activists took them to libraries, grade schools, elder communities and encouraged hands-on exploration.

As a result of this multitude of experiences, in the Berkeley campus grew the *Community Memory*, a project with the aim of fighting against the centralization of information technology for power and control purposes. The project consisted of a series of terminals linked to a central computer in San Francisco and scattered in public spaces available to the whole Berkeley community. The first terminal of *CM* was an ASR-33 teletype on a podium connected to a 110 baud modem, and was installed in August 1973 at *Leopold's Records*, a student-run record store in Berkeley (FIG. 16, 17). These terminals constituted the very first computerized bulletin board system, through which users within the Berkeley community could enter new messages or search for previously written ones.

The project was created by Efrem Lipkin, Mark Szpakowski

FIG. 15
Cover of *People's Computer Company*, Volume I, NO. I (October 1972).
Copyright: People's Computer Company. Source: computerhistory.org

FIG. 16
Model of community Memory terminal (1980 ca).
Copyright: Mark Richards.
Source: computerhistory.org

FIG. 17
Community Memory terminal at Leopold's Records (1975 ca).
Copyright: Unknown.
Source: computerhistory.org

and Lee Felsenstein, who operated under the name *Loving Grace Cybernetics* and whose ideals were deeply rooted in the countercultural movement of the late 1960s and early 1970s. The *Community Memory* presented a new and unique role for the computer, seen as a tool able to unhinge the passive and centralized information transmission of mass media by allowing a direct communication among citizens through a participative and computerized agora.

ARPA, together with universities, government agencies, corporates, and intellectuals, explored new paths in the field of computing that linked utopias, military purposes, and cutting-edge projects. All research and projects in particular shared the same, clear objective: the elaboration of a different, immediate, and intuitive way to interact with the machine, one where computers and networks were considered as relational environments and no longer as mere transmission channels.

Here one might start to understand *why* precisely in the 1960s the Kennedy-Nixon debate received such resonance: because, after a progressive change in scientific thinking started in the previous decade, the attention towards media shifted from their technical specificity to their potentiality as modeling tools for communication and interactivity[29]. Clearly, the experiences listed above do not exhaust the richness and diversity of the events and initiatives taking place in the U.S. of the late 1960s and early 1970s, nor the general complexity of the examined period. However, they tell us about the development of a new

---

[29] Although most of the texts and projects included in this section were developed between the late 1960s and early 1970s, it should be remembered that they were the result of a new scientific approach towards the fields of media and communication. In this regard, I should mention the influential communication model developed by Shannon and Weaver in 1948, which visualized a chain of transactional processes occurring during communication and, in making information measurable, gave birth to the mathematical study of information theory.

culture which contributed to turning the emergence of new media into a pretext to retroactively explore the effects of any media on society and citizens.

This shift in the conception of media is also what led computers and network technologies to be defined as *new* media. The specification 'new', in fact, has been used since the 1960s to describe changes in the field of media with regard to the interaction between users and the media and to the interaction among users themselves within a specific medium. Contrary to common belief, the 'new' in new media is neither intended in terms of technological advancement nor does it refer to devices released in a specific time frame. In fact, as technology continues to evolve, societies will constantly witness the emergence of 'new' kinds of media. Besides, if one were to consider media only in light of their techno-innovative aspects, the risk would be to underestimate the complexity of technology itself and the density of its *imaginaire*[30].

As Poster stresses, "the question of the new requires a historical problematic" where "the conceptual problem is to enable a historical differentiation of old and new without initiating a totalizing narrative"[31]. Eventually, one could say that the 'new' in new media can be understood as both a conception of the media that exceeds their mere technological specificities and focuses on their effects on society and individuals, as well as a constant redefinition process of the media system which actualizes in forms of hybridization between the 'new' and the 'old'. In this sense, the juxtaposition of 'new' with 'media' is used to indicate a paradigm shift in the conception of media that originated in the U.S. during the 1960s and is still evolving today.

[30] P. FLICHY, *The Internet Imaginaire* (Cambridge, MA: MIT Press, 2007).

[31] M. POSTER, *What's the Matter with the Internet?* (Minneapolis: University Of Minnesota Press, 2001), 12–13.

I hope that this brief digression into the word origin of new media is helpful to understand two main aspects that need to be taken into account when referring to them. First of all that, from an etymological point of view, the expression 'new media' refers both to new media as objects (i.e. in terms of their exhibiting, distribution, production, and storage abilities[32]) as well as means of communication – that is, as the set of rules, conventions, and organizational forms that people follow when using new media[33]. And secondly that, from a cultural perspective, new media were born under a schism between the idea of 'good media' and 'bad media'. In fact, as mentioned earlier, between the late 1960s and early 1970s computers were considered tools for democratic participation, weapons directed against technocracy, and icons of a new social order.

Alongside the projects discussed above, writings such as *Understanding Media* (1964), *Utopia or Oblivion* (1969), *Tools for Conviviality* (1973) and many others started to emphasize how new media would encourage people to think for themselves, be more socially engaged, and enable a harmonious development of society. These reflections led to the idea that this new man-machine-society triad could defeat the annihilating and degenerating society envisioned by 'bad' corporations and central governments, which embodied a form of centralization and control. Conviviality was the opposite of industrial, massified and alienating productivity controlled by the elite; and soon, this thinking added to a growing and fierce criticism against the Western cultural industry, its means of mass communication, and its persuasive and abusive power.

---

[32] L. MANOVICH, *The Language of New Media* (Cambridge, MA: MIT Press, 2001), 19.

[33] G. COSENZA, *Introduzione alla semiotica dei nuovi media* (Bari: Editori Laterza, 2014), 11.

HOPE AND DISTRUST

As highlighted throughout this chapter, the year 1960 heralded an important decade in Western history, distinguished by a series of great social, cultural and political events, and technological advancements which contributed to create a powerful shift within society. At the same time, the late 1960s and early 1970s marked the dispersal of design into the interdisciplinary realm of the social sciences, with a specific emphasis placed on experiential contexts, social imperatives and user needs that extended design practices to their furthest reaches. This is the case, for example, for the *First Things First* manifesto, written and published in 1964 by Ken Garland along with 20 other designers, photographers and students, which promoted the use of design for wider societal gain in contrast to the production of mainstream advertising.

Drawing on ideas shared by critical theorists, the Frankfurt School, the countercultural movements of the time, and various other influences, the manifesto explicitly reaffirmed the belief that design is not a neutral, value-free process, but rather a tool able to shape society at large. Driven by the changing relationship of design with politics, commerce and culture, the manifesto posed some profound questions and dilemmas regarding design education and practice, urging many practitioners in the following years to reflect on the consequences of their projects in terms of ecological and social change.

In the following decade, titles such as *Design for the Real World: Human Ecology and Social Change* (1971) by Victor Papanek and *Design, Nature, and Revolution: Toward a Critical Ecology* (1972) by Tomàs Maldonado represented – although very differently[34] – fundamental inquiries into the

---

[34] Even though both texts deal with a new approach to the design profession, understood as a tool operating outside the commodity culture and given economic structures, Papanek and Maldonado

role of design to a new generation of designers, particularly students, who demanded a more socially relevant agency and an end to modernist design *dicta*.

During this time, many communication designers – from independent figures (amateurs or professionals) to studios and even entire schools – merged with this cultural climate and, by questioning their role within society, started to extend the boundaries of their practice beyond commercial interests. In the U.S., political and social upheavals of the decade such as the Anti-Vietnam war movement, the fight for women's rights, and black people's liberation met powerful graphic expression and reclaimed the precious space of the streets, using posters as a tool to convey protest messages[35]. Similarly, in European countries, one can find many examples of how communication design was embedded in the social turmoil of the 1960s, adopting the poster in particular as a means to increase awareness of the fragility of civil and human rights, promote specific political parties, or force policy changes.

---

embodied radically different visions of this shift in design culture. For example, Papanek's perspective on design received fierce accusations of neocolonialism by some of his colleagues, who considered the intervention of Western designers in developing countries as patronizing and deeply harmful. Most notably, in 1974, Gui Bonsiepe (former Professor of the Ulm School of Design) accused Papanek of lacking basic political understandings of power relations, and of peddling a poisonous new brand of neocolonialism. Referring to Papanek's famous tin-can radio, Bonsiepe labeled it as a "paternalistic design – covered by humanitarian coating [...] doused in the ideology of the noble savage," as defined it as a tool for disseminating pro-American propaganda throughout largely non-literate countries (see Gui Bonsiepe, "Design and Under-development," Casabella 385, January (1974): 43).

[35] The use of posters as a means of political expression during the late 1960s represented a novelty aspect to American politics, also because, in the previous decade, the strictness and conformity caused by the deterrent effect of the Cold War in combination with McCarthyism made it too dangerous to produce political content for public spaces.

Of particular importance among these are the students and teachers of Atelier Populaire who, in the spring of 1968, decided to occupy the studios of the École des Beaux-Arts in Paris – already on strike – to produce posters in support of the great movement of striking workers who were occupying factories in defiance of the Gaullist government. Unlike any other design created for political purposes in the past, at Atelier Populaire neither the conception nor the production process depended on propaganda departments or professionals alone: anyone involved in the cause could contribute to originate the message of posters and control the means of production.

As stated in a booklet edited by students of the École des Beaux-Arts in 1968, at Atelier Populaire everyone – "worker or student, foreign or French" – could come and participate in the enthusiasm of the posters production, and workers especially were invited to "propose slogans, discuss with artists and students, criticize the posters produced or distribute them outside"[36]. Each night, between May 14 and June 27, 1968, at 64 Rue du Richelieu, the poster projects were submitted anonymously and discussed at general assemblies according to the correctness of the political message and the way the it was conveyed[37]. This participatory *modus operandi* allowed many players involved in the strikes to participate in the vibrant atmosphere of Atelier Populaire alongside workers, from French Communist Party members to Situationists, Enragés, and intellectuals. After posters were collectively analyzed and voted on, the accepted projects were realized in the lithography studio by teams working in shifts around the clock.

If one is to analyze the production of Atelier Populaire from a formal perspective, it can be noted that most posters were

---

[36] U.U.U., L'atelier populaire présenté par lui-même (Self-published, 1968), 10. Translation by the author.
[37] IBID.

produced with the use of the opaque projector and silkscreen. This choice should not be underestimated, considering that students of the École des Beaux-Arts were only familiar with mediums such as lithography and offset printing. Silkscreen printing – which was not taught at fine arts schools and was infrequently used by French artists at that time – was introduced at Atelier Populaire by painter and sculptor Guy de Rougemont.

After studying at the École des arts décoratifs in Paris from 1954 to 1958 and living from time to time in New York during the 1960s, de Rougemont came back to Paris in 1968 and proposed the use of silkscreen at Atelier Populaire during the assembly of May 14. In the following days, he set up the screen printing studio in the lithography studio at the Paris École des Beaux-Arts with Eric Seydoux – who also lived in New York between 1963 and 1967 and returned to Paris to pursue professional silkscreen printing.

As art historian and critic Liam Considine suggests, the use of silkscreen highlights a "processes of transatlantic cultural transfer as well as the politicization of art during the events of May 1968"[38]. In fact, although many French critics were doubtful about pop art's mechanization of painterly techniques, it became a means of expression brought about by force of circumstance. Due to the pace of the events of the uprising, the artists and students who established the Atelier Populaire strayed from traditional *beaux-arts* mediums, deeming the expediency of silkscreen the best way to spread messages in a moment of political crisis.

Furthermore, in order to accelerate the production of posters and create poster workshops in occupied factories as well[39], Atelier Populaire produced and distributed a text detailing the steps of the silkscreen printing process. This way of working,

[38] L. CONSIDINE, "Screen Politics: Pop Art and the Atelier Populaire – Tate Papers," *Tate Papers*, NO. 24 (Autumn 2015).
[39] L. GERVEREAU, "Les affiches de 'mai 68,'" *Matériaux pour l'histoire de notre temps* II, NO. I (1988): 160–71.

similarly to an assembly line, was a deliberate connection with labor[40]: Atelier Populaire rejected the elevation of artists above workers, and pointed instead at the centrality of the silkscreen as an identitarian medium which – precisely because of its replicability – could keep the problems of the working class at the center of their objectives.

FIG. 18
Atelier Populaire, *Usines Universités Union* (1968). Copyright: Bibliothèque nationale de France. Source: gallica.bnf.fr

This replicable model of screen printing production also allowed Atelier Populaire to inspire many other self-managed workshops in Western countries that crafted posters for political purposes, such as the Poster Workshop in Camden Town[41] and the Berkeley Political Protest Workshop[42]. "Far from a neu-

---

[40] The first lithographic poster produced at Atelier Populaire headlined *Usines, Universités, Union* (Factories, Universities, Union), signaling the unity between workers and students and their mutual solidarity (FIG. 18).

[41] The Poster Workshop (1968-1971) was a screen printing collective founded in 1968 and operating in a basement in Camden, London. Run entirely by volunteers, it fulfilled a need for the creation and print of posters by the many different groups who were planning demonstrations and protests in London, from council tenants and factory workers to liberation movements and student associations.

[42] In May 1970, students at the University of California, Berkeley, came together to form the Berkeley Political Poster Workshop, which produced hundreds of silk screen designs. Under the guidance of Malaquias Montoya, a leading figure of the Chicano Art Movement, students created vivid and colorful images of resistance in response to the

tral medium", says Considine, "the industriousness of the silk-screen enabled the conceptualisation of the studio as a factory, and of posters as a form of counter-media able to respond to and shape the events"[43].

Throughout time, Atelier Populaire became also a clear example of how the world of communication design was merging with the intellectual movements that warned against the tendency of the media to divert attention from the practical goals of politics. Not surprisingly, explicit reference to Guy Debord's theory of "the Spectacle" was often a main theme in their posters and causes. In particular, after the workers at ORTF[44] went on strike on May 20, 1968, Atelier Populaire produced a series of designs denouncing the control over French television – and especially news broadcasts – exercised by the national government. For example, in in *Libérons l'O.R.T.F* ('Let's Free O.R.T.F.'), a character is depicted between the bars of a television wearing a phrygian cap – the hat worn by freed slaves in ancient Rome and later by American and French revolutionaries (FIG. 19).

FIG. 19
Atelier Populaire, *Libérons l'O.R.T.F* (1968). Copyright: Bibliothèque nationale de France. Source: gallica.bnf.fr

increasing political tumults, from Nixon's ordered bombing of Cambodia to the Kent State shootings occurred just days before the workshop.
[43] CONSIDINE, "Screen Politics."
[44] The Office de Radiodiffusion-Télévision Française (ORTF) was the national agency charged with providing public radio and television in France between 1964 and 1974.

Instead, in *La voix de son maître* ('His Master's Voice'), a television is held between the hands of a character with a kepi – a hat commonly associated with French military and police uniforms (FIG. 20).

FIG. 20
Atelier Populaire, *La voix de son maître* (1968). Copyright: Bibliothèque nationale de France. Source: gallica.bnf.fr

As television and radio broadcasts began to show hostility to workers' uprisings, the antagonistic position of Atelier Populaire towards French mainstream media escalated even further. In particular, during the third week of strikes the poster became a crucial expression of emancipation against television. To the cries of *On vous intoxique!* (You Are Being Poisoned!) and *Toute la presse est toxique* (All press is toxic), Atelier Populaire turned the poster into a bulletin titled *Journal Mural* to spread their own narratives about the ongoing events (FIG. 21, 22, 23). Produced between 13 and 21 June, 1968, the *Journal Mural* was both stuck on walls as well as circulated among strikers and civilians in the streets of Paris, becoming an essential medium for the dissemination of news. If the state had television to project its views into people's homes, students had the streets to put their case as effectively as possible.

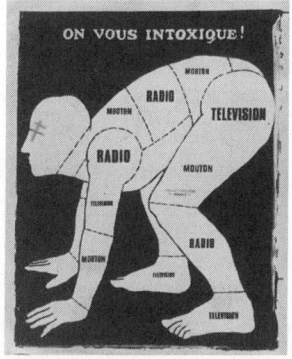

FIG. 21
Atelier Populaire, *On vous intoxique!* (1968) Copyright: Bibliothèque nationale de France. Source: gallica.bnf.fr

FIG. 22
Atelier Populaire, *Toute la presse est toxique* (1968). Copyright: Bibliothèque nationale de France. Source: gallica.bnf.fr

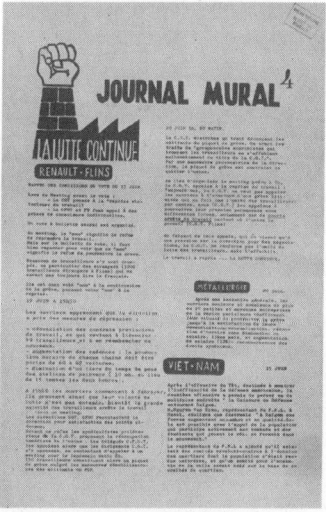

FIG. 23
Atelier Populaire, *Journal Mural* (1968). Copyright: Bibliothèque nationale de France. Source: gallica.bnf.fr

In the same years, in Italy, the poster represented the quintessential medium in political communication, providing political movements with strong visual characterization through the use of color, shapes, and emblems[45]. This is the case of many Italian designers such as Michele Spera, Ettore Vitale, Bruno Magno, and many others who, with their prolific poster production, provided parties such as the PRI (Italian Republican Party), PSI (Italian Socialist Party), and PCI (Italian Communist Party) with strong visual characterizations (FIG. 24, 25, 26).

Possibly one the most important and innovative features of these works was the use of coordinated systems of graphic elements, which represented yet another unseen approach in the Western political scenario between the fields of political communication and corporate identity. This aspect allowed PRI, PSI, and PCI to be easily recognizable by citizens, whilst simultaneously assigning a strong political and social role to the design profession. As scholar Luciano Cheles notices, the Italian political posters of the late 1960s and early 1970s were seemingly unaffected by the images produced by new political and countercultural movements such as the Cuban revolution, French May '68, and anti-Vietnam protest movements[46].

Since all parties' communication materials were developed under commissioned work, the poster "fulfilled a more generic and allusive function", reminding "what a given party stood for, often using a subtle and even playful idiom that addressed itself to a selected audience – one made up largely by sympa-

---

[45] Also, until the mid-1970s, posters were for Italian opposition parties a crucial means for making their views known to the general public, as a large part of the press and state-owned broadcasting service were biased in favor of the ruling coalition.

[46] L. CHELES, "Picture battles in the piazza: the political poster," in *The Art of Persuasion: Political Communication in Italy from 1945 to the 1990s*, ed. Luciano Cheles and Lucio Sponza (Manchester: Manchester University Press, 2001), 143.

FIG. 24
Michele Spera, *Tesseramento* (1965).
Copyright: Michele Spera.
Source: designculture.it

FIG. 25
Ettore Vitale, *25 Aprile* (1973).
Copyright: ISMEL. Source: ismel.it

FIG. 26
Bruno Magno, *Sparano alla democrazia*
(1970 ca). Copyright: Bruno Magno.
Source: B. Magno, *Vedere a sinistra:
Bruno Magno dal PCI al PDS : i
manifesti e altre immagini 1971/1991*
(Editori riuniti, 1991).

thizers"⁴⁷. Because of their different *raison d'être*, these posters aimed at looking more professional and attractive rather than being used as means of dialectic exchange such as those produced at the silk-screen printing workshop of Atelier Populaire. What is also interesting to note about the production of these posters is that, as Cheles points out, "despite the growing interest in the verbal and visual codes of commercial advertising" that permeated most of Western political communication, almost no Italian party "entrusted its campaign to an external agency"⁴⁸. Indeed, communication material within the Italian political scene was traditionally produced by the parties' propaganda departments or by graphic designers politically close to them.

This skepticism, according to Cheles, might also be related to an 'incident' concerning a campaign promoted by DC (Democrazia Cristiana, 'Christian Democracy') close to the Italian general elections of 1963. This year is extremely important in the history of Italian politics, because in addition to marking the entry of the Socialists into the government, it signaled a major advance by the Communist Party in electoral preferences (an aspect that was later reflected in the vote at the ballot box).

To best prepare for the elections, DC campaign director Adolfo Sarti commissioned the Institute for Motivational Research to conduct a survey on how to set up the party's election campaign⁴⁹. The head of the American agency was Ernest Dichter, psychologist and father of many significantly influential practices in the advertising industry of the early 20th century. Dichter and his agency conducted an analysis of the party to improve its communication, concluding that DC was a "disregarded party" with an aura of "passivity and old age". To try and solve this

[47] IBID, 144.
[48] IBID, 141.
[49] E. NOVELLI, *Le campagne elettorali in Italia. Protagonisti, strumenti, teorie* (Bari: Laterza, 2018), 79.

image problem, Dichter's studio produced a poster featuring a young woman with a bouquet of flowers and the slogan *'La DC ha vent'anni'* (DC is twenty years old). As Cheles recounts, "Its consequences were disastrous: all over Italy the posters invited graffiti," amongst which *'Allora bisogna farle la festa'* ('Let's cut them off then') and *'È ora di fotterla'* ('Then it's time to fuck her')[50]. The so-called *Rapporto Dichter* ('Dichter Report') ended up becoming a scandal, and many strongly criticized the DC for involving in the dynamics of Italian politics the "American persuaders" – a term dubbed by journalist Rubens Tedeschi within an article in L'Unità, a leading newspaper of the Italian left (FIG. 27).

FIG. 27
Article from the Italian left-wing oriented newspaper *L'unità*, written by Rubens Tedeschi. March 15, 1968, p. 3.

As the Italian sociologist and journalist Edoardo Novelli points out, it is possible that DC's poor electoral outcome in the 1963 elections ended up curbing the process of fusion between politics and advertisement[51] – a system already widely established in the United States as well as in other European countries. "The superficial lesson that parties evince[d] from this history," writes Novelli, "is that elections are not won thanks to polls and foreign consultants"[52]. This feeling of distrust, as Cheles reports in his research, can also be traced long after 1963. For example,

---

[50] CHELES, "Picture battles in the piazza: the political poster," 141.
[51] NOVELLI, *Le campagne elettorali in Italia*, 76.
[52] IBID.

in an interview for Budget magazine held in 1968, the co-director of the PSI propaganda department Michele Pellicani expresses great reluctanctoward political advertisement, going so far as to state that:

> "To impose an ideology, a political program, or a party, the 'persuader' must himself be persuaded, whereas he can succeed in selling a bar of soap or a bouillon cube without believing that they are good. Of course, the issue of advertisement techniques also exists for parties, but this does not solve the problem of propaganda, which for parties is based on the strength of ideals"[53].

This quote is especially important because it reflects a view that would be endorsed until the beginning of the following decade (and not just in Italy) by many other parties that deemed the posters produced by communication designers more pertinent to the representation of political ideals compared to political commercials produced by advertisers. However, as seen with Eisenhower's TV ads produced by Rosser Reeves, advertising strategies became increasingly integrated with and applied to politics. And, as in the case of Kennedy, politicians themselves began to understand more and more the social logics underpinning visual media and the culture industry.

Although Italian politics initially 'rejected' the union of politics and marketing, the introduction of advertising techniques in the Western political world soon ushered in a period where citizens, just like consumers, were presented through mass media with a wide range of politicians from which they could select. Against this background, communication designers in the U.S. sought ways of engagement between the fields of

[53] L. SOLLAZZO, "Pubblicità Elettorale," *Sipradue,* December 1968, 27–28. Translation by the author.

communication design and political communication that did not involve close cooperation with a specific political party. For example, in the *Give a Damn* campaign designed by Stephen O. Frankfurt and his advertising agency Young & Rubicam (FIG. 28, 29), communication design was used to shed light on social injustices in the City of New York by blanketing the city with graphics – although in a very different way than Atelier Populaire did. The *Give a Damn* campaign was initiated by the New York Urban Coalition, created 1967 by John Lindsay – the mayor of New York City at that time – and consisting of partners from law firms, business leaders, and activists. As a socially liberal Republican, Lindsay supported many cultural

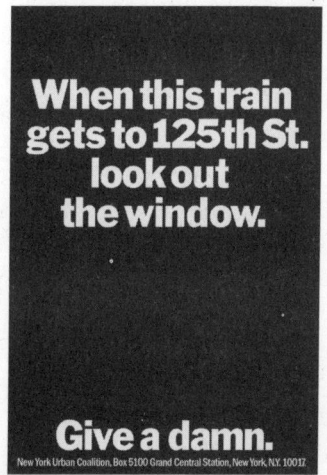

FIG. 28
Stephen Frankfurt, *Give a Damn* Campaign. Subway poster, New York (1968). Copyright: Unknown. Source: Museum of the City of New York, Prints & Photographs Collection.

FIG. 29
Stephen Frankfurt, *Give a Damn* Campaign. Poster, New York (1968). Copyright: Unknown. Source: Museum of the City of New York.

and humanitarian initiatives, and the NYUC became a way to support the needs of urban ghetto residents by assisting with children's education, adult job training, aid to minority businesses, and help dealing with unscrupulous landlords and rising rents. The campaign included the production of newspaper ads, advertising in subways, pins, and posters designed by Stephen O. Frankfurt, but also one TV ad and a song entitled *Give a Damn* written by Bob Dorough and Stu Scharf and recorded by Spanky and Our Gang, released 'as a public service' by Mercury Records.

The brief stir surrounding *Give a Damn* and the social movement it supported may seem insignificant compared to all that transpired in 1968. But by examining it we are treated to a microcosm of the forces that were at work in the U.S. of 1968: the forces that were spinning the country in a new direction and those that tried to keep that direction from becoming reality.

Both the *Give a Damn* campaign and the Italian political posters of the late 1960s and early 1970s hold a special place in the history of communication design, as they gave a concrete answer to designers' need to think beyond the commercial uses of design. Specifically, they demonstrated how design professionals alone or even entire communication agencies could turn design into a useful service to create a more informed, active, and conscious citizenry.

However, because of their dependency on public administrations and political parties' commissions, these kinds of design interventions could become real opportunities only in light of specific and fortunate circumstances. Unlike Atelier Populaire and the other screen printing workshops, the design of these social campaigns and of posters for political parties was necessarily promoted by the managers of the *res publica*, and thus remained confined to specific favorable political timeframes.

Nevertheless, new hybrid spaces of production emerged for designers willing to engage in socio-political issues. At Esquire magazine, for example, American art director George Lois designed ninety-two covers using powerful photographs and photomontages to make succinct editorial statements about the United States from the 1960s to the early 1970s. Different from other U.S. magazines at that time, Esquire covers were generally poster-like and free of excess words, acting as independent visual and verbal statements about topics often related to politics and civil rights. With the help of photographer Carl Fischer, Lois used humor and spot-on visual references as weapons to make graphic commentaries which eventually became memorable icons of that unsettling social and political era. In particular, two memorable and iconic covers became those of April and May 1968.

The first depicted boxer Muhammed Ali riddled with six arrows as a modern St. Sebastian, in a photo that shocked readers for many reasons (FIG. 30). Not only was the 'mighty' Ali portrayed as fallible, bleeding from six wounds and mouth agape in agony, but the image was also loaded with allusions to highly charged events rippling through and dividing America. Lois and Fischer shot the photo in late 1967, when tensions from the civil rights movement and Vietnam War protests ran high. Ali, then in his mid-twenties, fought for both causes and therefore became a galvanizing example of black triumph after winning the heavyweight championship in 1964.

However, due to his conversion to Islam in 1964, Ali refused to be drafted into the Army – a move that made him enemies across government, sports, publishing, and American households. In response, Ali was stripped of his heavyweight title, and his boxing license was revoked from the time he was twenty-five until he was almost twenty-nine years old – the prime of a boxer's physicality. He was fined $10,000 and later arrested, though he never served time (he was cleared by the U.S. Supreme Court in 1971). By 1965, every action taken by Muhammad Ali was interpreted in terms not only of his boxing talent, but also of his religious convictions. Indeed, his decision to refuse conscription into the military gave him a new public persona as a war resister whose actions might affect those of other young black men. Portrayed as an iconic third-century martyr, Ali transcended his prior selves as the

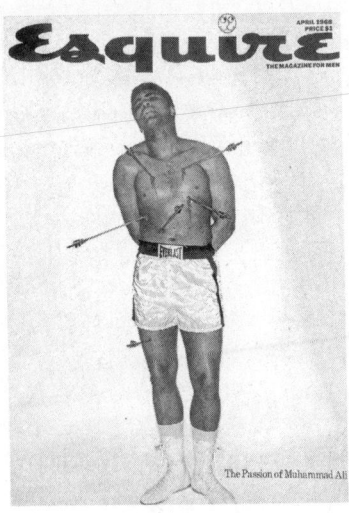

FIG. 30
Esquire Vol. 69, NO. 6, *The Passion of Muhamad Ali* (April 1968). Copyright: Esquire. Source: classic.esquire.com

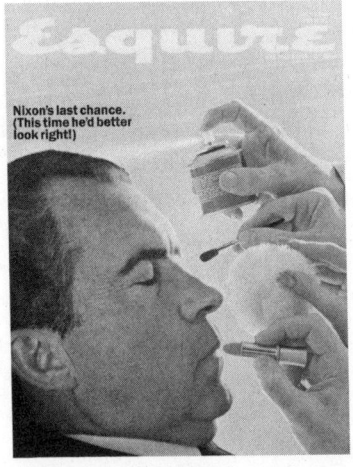

FIG. 31
Esquire Vol. 69, NO. 7, *Nixon's last chance* (May 1968). Copyright: Esquire. Source: classic.esquire.com

brash and plucky challenger and the champion with the unpopular religious choice. Through Esquire's cover of April 4, 1968[54], the glorious boxer eventually became a symbol for the rejection of governmental authority and the idol of a generation struggling for basic human rights.

The second cover produced by Lois depicts Richard Nixon being doused in make-up and hairspray, accompanied by the statement "Nixon's last chance. (This time he'd better look right!)" (FIG. 31). The cover ironically alludes to the famous televised debate held in September 1960 between Nixon and Kennedy, when Nixon was undoubtedly less prepared – or at least incapacitated[55] – compared to Kennedy for a TV appearance.

The cover was released five months prior to the U.S. presidential elections of 1968, when Nixon was running for his second term. Driven by an ongoing need to prove himself, he brought a 'new Nixon' into the 1968 race for president, portraying himself as an older, wiser, and more statesmanlike version of the combative anticommunist that characterized his former candidacy. However, by referring to the theory of Kennedy's alleged 'victory' during the debate of 1960, Lois revived the memory of a sweaty and stumped Nixon – an image which he had tried to erase for most of his 1968 campaign. At the same time, after less than a year since the publication of Debord's *La société du spectacle*, the cover symbolized the critique on the current state of political communication, merging with contemporary consumer culture and favoring appearance over content.

The examples shown so far demonstrate how communication design was able, despite its commercial nature, to comment

---

[54] The day the Esquire cover hit newsstands Martin Luther King Jr. was assassinated, endowing the image with even deeper significance, and highlighting themes of racial persecution and peaceful protest.

[55] In addition to avoiding makeup, Nixon was still recovering from a painful knee injury that occurred during a campaign trail in North Carolina which caused him to appear sallow and underweight.

critically on current social events and reach a fairly wide audience. However, between the late 1960s and early 1970s, design also began to intertwine with the art world through the experiences of visionary curators who foresaw the role of designers as channellers of current political, economical, and social changes. In this sense, the game-changing group show *Information*, curated by Kynaston McShine in 1970 at MoMa, became a significant exhibition precisely due to its focus on new modes of communication and its emphasis on data and information over aesthetics and visual pleasure.

The exhibition contains the works of nearly one hundred U.S. and European artists whose objecthood in most cases is stripped to the bone, leading McShine to open up a profound reflection on the materiality of art, which is reduced to pure concept and information exchange. On display were Christine Kozlov's telegram addressed to the curator, images transmitted via telex by the Canadian collective N.E. Thing Co., and many other artifacts that showed how the speed, storage and exchange of information constituted crucial elements in yet another transformation of the contemporary art landscape.

Undoubtedly, *Information* was one of the first attempts by a major art institution to showcase the increasingly emerging artistic strategies now categorized as Conceptualism. However, alongside this brave choice in McShine's curatorship, art and design curator Jeremiah McCarthy suggests that *Information* is possibly the first exhibition where design played a major role by providing the tools to visualize the "institutional critique" typical of conceptual art. Specifically, in his thesis *The Artist and the "Information" Machine: Conceptualism, Technology, and Design in 1970*, McCarthy examines Ettore Sottsass's Jukebox by highlighting its importance within the larger concept of the exhibition. With forty standing stations, Sottsass' Jukebox was presented as a giant flying saucer where spectators could place their heads in individual helmets equipped with two integrated speakers, and look at ten short movies projected on a loop one after the other. What is interesting, however, is that Sottsass' Jukebox was initially conceived in 1968 for Olivetti's monumental *Concept and form* exhibition, with the aim of displaying films showcasing the variety, history, and quality of their products. For all intents and purposes, although groundbreaking in its design, Sottsass' Jukebox was a project designed to be used for representative exhibitions or business fairs[56] (FIG. 32).

FIG. 32
Sottsass' Jukebox in a showroom in Turin (1968). Copyright: Associazione Archivio Storico Olivetti/Publifoto. Source: storiaolivetti.it

The critical nature of this object, then, lies in the context in which it is presented, that is a strongly politicized exhibition such as *Information*. The choice to include an object designed for commercial purposes within an exhibition intended to pursue a form of somewhat blatant institutional critique unveils a critical tension between the field of design and arts, and the corporate and productive one.

As we saw in the previous section, technology and particularly new media were at a crossroads with respect to their future, which included either their incorporation into commercial and privatized systems, or their explosion into a new global community system. At a time when artists and designers were witnessing an epochal shift that would forever change the relationship

[56] J. W. MCCARTHY, "The Artist and the 'Information' Machine: Conceptualism, Technology, and Design in 1970" (New York, CUNY Hunter College, 2016), 14.

between corporations and practitioners, McShine tackles the issue head-on by putting a corporate propaganda machine in the museum, paving the way for reflection on who will be the information holders in the future.

McCarthy argues that even the catalog of the exhibition had the same purpose: to address the interconnectedness of the term *Information* and its relation to technology, and to expose its criticalities through visual means. At times where the role of design and art within this new technological realm was yet to be imagined, the cover of the *Information* catalog designed by Michael Lauretano seems to function as a visual essay that seeks to answer these questions (FIG. 33).

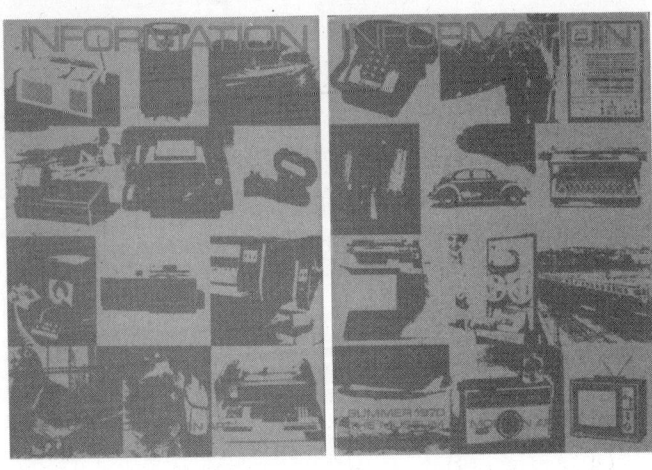

FIG. 33
Michael Lauretano, Catalog of *Information* (1970). Copyright: Kynaston L. McShine, Michael Lauretano. Source: The Museum of Modern Art Archives.

Across the front and back cover, a series of technological objects (a telephone, a Volkswagen Beetle, an Olivetti Praxis 48 typewriter, a television, a Boeing 747, and more) are placed in a grid and blended together through a series of dots, which resemble the distinctive pattern of photomechanical prints under magnification. With this technique, details fade away in favor of a pattern of interrelated objects which depicted the most advanced communication technologies at the time. This matrix of objects is put under scrutiny almost like the biopsy of a tissue, where the objects are both witnesses of a new form of materiality as well as a complex tapestry of meaning which is yet to be unfolded.

Through McShine's curatorship we witness an inquiry into the aesthetic canons generated by technology and media, coupled with an earnest reflection on the repercussions that these new devices may elicit both in society and in the art field. *Information* leaves the sphere of computer science and engineering and penetrates the empty spaces left by Lauretano's dotted cover, giving rise to a dense mass ready to shape new communities and new conflicts.

Once again, we are faced with an experience which displays both demise and redemption. The liberatory capacities of new media are confronted with an uncanny mesh of visible and invisible agents which are slowly dragging art, design and corporations into an unforeseeable and tense relationship. The alienating industrial productivity and the despicable military forces against which the 1968 generation lashed out so fiercely were present in the exhibition, although not entirely visible. They were hidden in the tight meshes of the *Information* exhibition cover, joining design and art in a grip that would make it increasingly difficult to separate in the world of media the good from the bad, the moral from the immoral – the hope from distrust.

WEATHER REPORT NR. I

As we have seen with the case study of the Kennedy-Nixon debate, the 1960s inaugurated the development of a new kind of political image on the Western political scene. Politicians increasingly relied on advertising agencies to produce TV ads to set out their political agenda, but also used the medium of television to promote (or amplify) their own self-image. This shift did not only permanently alter the systems of political representation, but also contributed to affirming visual communication as a fundamental dimension of political activity through the work of many scholars who began to research the role of images and media over political processes.

In this scenario, communication design started to move away from the conception of propaganda widely put into use in the first half of the 20th century and began to experiment with new ways of engaging with socio-political issues. Designers, art directors, curators and many other creative professionals came up with new ways to connect citizens with politics, providing the first with accessible production systems, or making them question their relationship with corporations and institutions. In years when television predominated over any other medium and the 'communication industries' (public relations, marketing and advertising) were becoming increasingly important, communication designers in Western countries came closer to the printing process in the most surprising challenge to technical advancements and electronic media. In particular, the poster became one of the main mediums with which political stances were made – whether produced for protests, political parties, or social campaigns.

On the one hand, Atelier Populaire and the other silk-screen printing workshops showed how independent and self-organized groups of people could take control of the printing process, strengthening the idea of community, network, and knowledge-sharing derived by countercultures and cybercultures in the U.S. Meanwhile, advertising agencies in the U.S. and other Western countries started a series of prolific collaborations with the political world, changing unimaginably the field of political communication.

But communication designers sought also other forms of engagement between the fields of communication design and political communication that went beyond the close cooperation with a specific political party or social movement. In Lois's case, for example, it is possible to observe how advertising and communication design came to a critical point where the art director used a mass medium to inform, entertain, alter or challenge citizen's beliefs and assumptions on a specific topic, and – paradoxically – to even comment on advertising's hypocrisy. And, with *Information*, design was implemented into the exhibition system and played a major role in providing the tools to *visualize* both the oppressive and liberatory capacities of technology, exposing its criticalities through visual means.

Overall, the episodes mentioned in this chapter are only a small part of a larger confluence of events which caused the fields of new media technologies and political communication to intertwine, giving life to a cataclysmic force able to turn the tide of Western democracies: the Superstorm.

At this initial stage the Superstorm is still malleable, fueled by the development of hopes and fears with regard to the future of Western politics and thus very open to conflicting interpretations on its nature. On one hand, most of the academic and intellectual thinking in the second half of the 20th century fed a 'pessimistic' perception over the role of images and media within Western societies, convinced that the aestheticization processes triggered by the encounter of the two would lead to a degradation of rationality in the political realm, and turn citizens into passive and alienated spectators. On the other hand, many activists from the worlds of cybercultures brought forward the idea of a dichotomous division between 'good' media – identified mainly as the computer and the internet, which were considered tools for democratic participation, weapons against technocracy, and icons of a new social order – and 'bad' media – that is any form of centralized media industry which embodied the controlling and manipulative power of the central state.

And still, in the midst of all these uncertainties, the Superstorm manifested itself thanks to the attention paid, although expressed in very different ways, towards images and their role within the shaping of future political and social imaginaries. In fact, in those years, the role of images acquired an increasing importance dictated by the diffusion of television in Western households, the widespread use of DIY printing systems, and a number of other means of communication which allowed new and different ways of conveying political and social messages. We can see the trace of the Superstorm in the choice of Kennedy to put makeup on before a televised debate, in the collectivization of printing processes, in the warnings issued by Debord and various members of the Frankfurt School, but also in the Community Memory terminal at Leopold's Records and on the cover of MoMa's 1970 exhibition's catalog *Information*. In this complex and multifaceted scenario, three aspects have become increasingly clear. The first one is that, between the 1960s and early 1970s, the emergence of new media technologies and the advancement achieved in the field of political communication allowed these two fields to become synergetic forces able to galvanize a wide range of debates which added to the complex zeitgeist of those years.

The second aspect is that the Superstorm manifested itself through the attention expressed by intellectuals, activists and scholars towards visual communication and more precisely towards the power of images to shape the Western social and political landscape. And the last aspect is that communication designers, faced with great societal challenges, started to demand a more politically relevant agency to their practice. Whether through the collaboration with a specific party, the use of design as a tool for scrutiny and judgment of the current political climate, the planning of social campaigns, or the inclusion of one or more design objects in exhibitions about the future of technology, designers began scouring the ground in search of new directions to make their way into the Superstorm.

II
ANATOMY OF THE SUPERSTORM.
DESIGN ISSUES IN A MEDIATIZED WORLD

As we have seen in chapter one, the 1960s and early 1970s filled the future of new media with a plentiful series of predictions – both positive and negative. On the one hand, the utopian forces that drove the countercultural movements in the U.S. and across Europe in that period foresaw the potential of new media to exceed the militaristic nature of technologies and facilitate the creation of new social relations. In a historical moment marked by geopolitical conflicts and the threat of a nuclear war, authors such as Buckminister Fuller, Marshall McLuhan and Ivan Illich, together with Western youth movements, forged a cybernetic notion of the globe as a single, interlinked system of information that was deeply reassuring.

More than twenty years later, the same machines born under the sign of Cold War's technocracy and filled with the hopes of cybercultures seemed finally ready to bring to life the countercultural dream of empowered individualism, collaborative community, and spiritual communion. On the other hand, the harsh critiques brought forward by the Frankfurt School's scholars and many other European intellectuals since the 1960s inspired further concerns regarding the effects of media on political and social processes.

In particular, many scholars in communication and media studies continued to express their disquiet towards the increasing aestheticization of the political realm, constantly questioning the role of images and media in relation to the representation of everyday and institutional politics. However, as the personal computer and the World Wide Web entered the Western world, the 1990s presented themselves as a new terrain onto which new theories could be written. In particular, the increasing importance of images in the ever-mediated political scene prompted more and more scholars to abandon their radical positions on new media (whether good or bad) and give progressively more space to new perspectives in media studies. This change is mainly highlighted by the academic shift towards the "pictorial turn", a term introduced notably by media researcher W. J. T. Mitchell in the homonymous article published in the magazine *Artforum* in 1992.

The pictorial turn emerged in academia as a reaction to a series of important transformations that occurred since the beginning of the 1990s in the field of images. In the first place it is important to notice how, with the development of the internet, the progressive diffusion of wireless network technology and the increasingly easy access to softwares and devices for the production, storage, and sharing of images, the number of circulated images rose dramatically.

Another key aspect for the development of the pictorial turn was that, since the mid-1990s, many broadcasters started to build transnational TV networks which allowed them to have a larger reach and therefore gain an increasingly globalized audience. In a scenario where most national broadcaster's signal covered only the events occurring within national borders, the evolution of cross-border television channels brought about the global dissemination of images of great political and social impact, able to profoundly affect the collective imagination of the "global village" foreseen by McLuhan. In fact, as highlighted by visual culture experts Antonio Somaini and Andrea Pinotti in their book *Cultura visuale. Immagini sguardi media dispositivi*,

> "media made visible, and live, historical events charged with a strong political, social and emo-

> tional impact – such as the fall of the Berlin Wall in
> 1989, the bombardment in Baghdad broadcasted
> by CNN in 1990, the cannon fires against the Russian Parliament in 1993, the crowd attending the
> funeral of Lady Diana in 1997, and the worldwide
> broadcast of the images displaying the attack on
> the World Trade Center on September 11, 2001"[57].

The ever-increasing number of circulating images and the emergence of new tools for the visualization of information have given rise to a great interest for the role of the visual into specific disciplines that had never considered images as an object of study. It was between the late 1980s and the early 1990s, in fact, that the academic world began to inquire into the documentary, testimonial and archival role of images, thus highlighting their peculiar anthropological value.

With the pictorial turn, images started to be conceived not only as instruments of manipulation, but also as independent sources with their own objectives and meanings. From the 1990s onwards, the visual sphere and its culture started to be investigated as mediators of social interactions, as a repertoire of values and models that structure and filter the ways humans read and decipher reality.

The pictorial turn can be read as a consequence of – or as a parallel phenomenon to – the so-called process of mediatization, a concept introduced in the fields of media and communication theory in approximately the same years[58]. The term mediatiza-

---

[57] A. PINOTTI AND A. SOMAINI, *Cultura visuale. Immagini, sguardi, media, dispositivi* (Torino: Einaudi, 2016), 19–20.

[58] As is often the case, the concept of 'mediatization' did not just *appear* in the 1990s. Many scholarly discourses had already been developing it decades earlier, but never through a precise strand of literature, nor referring specifically to the term 'mediatization'. In their article *Conceptualizing Mediatization: Contexts, Traditions, Arguments*

tion was born to denote the intensified and changing importance of media in culture and society, and many scholars used it as a concept to read the effects of a particular medium in different historical socio-cultural processes[59]. According to media scholars Friedrich Krotz and Andreas Hepp, mediatization can be considered as an investigative approach to media that allows us to understand how a new medium gives life to great changes in one's daily life.

Specifically, mediatization is a process through which culture and society become increasingly dependent and intertwined with the 'media logic' of a specific medium. The term media logic constitutes a key pillar behind the process of mediatization, and is often regarded as a conceptual shorthand used by scholars to define the institutional, aesthetic and technological *modus operandi* of a specific medium[60]. This includes the ways

---

(2013), media scholars Nick Couldry and Andreas Hepp suggest that mediatization gained many different meanings in social and cultural research throughout history. Specifically, they argue that the emergence of this concept can be dated back to the early 20th century, with Ernst Manheim's postdoctoral thesis *The bearers of public opinion* (1933), and was later developed further in the works of Jean Baudrillard (1981), Jürgen Habermas (1984) and Ulf Hannerz (1990). In their works, the authors refer to media in different manners, and attribute even more varied values to the concept of mediatization. Yet, the reason they all converge in Couldry and Hepp's list of mediatization theorists is their shared vision of mediatization *as a way to decipher change*.

[59] D. L. ALTHEIDE AND R.P. SNOW, *Media Logic* (Los Angeles: SAGE, 1979); Stig Hjarvard, "The Mediatization of Society," *Nordicom Review* 29, NO. 2 (November 1, 2008): 102–31; J. STRÖMBÄCK, "Four Phases of Mediatization: An Analysis of the Mediatization of Politics," *The International Journal of Press/Politics* 13, NO. 3 (July 1, 2008): 228–46.

[60] D. L. ALTHEIDE, "Media Logic," in *The International Encyclopedia of Political Communication* (American Cancer Society, 2016), 1–6; F. ESSER, "Mediatization as a Challenge: Media Logic Versus Political Logic," in *Democracy in the Age of Globalization and Mediatization*, ed. Hanspeter Kriesi et al. (London: Palgrave Macmillan UK, 2013), 155–76.

in which media distribute material and symbolic resources and how they come to institutionalize new forms of social interaction or change existing ones when applied to a specific field. For example, when political parties started to hire professionals with expertise in social media networks, they not only acquired the ability to project political messages through social media platforms, but also introduced new kinds of logic into the political realm itself (i.e. the increase in the amount and speed of the visual content to be produced, its aesthetic and formal qualities, and so on).

Similarly, when designers faced the introduction of new softwares such as Photoshop or Indesign, a whole new set of principles and logics replaced the existing systems of image-making – thus relentlessly changing the design profession. And, with the rapid growth of the professional figures associated with the development of political images, the role and scope of designers within the political and social sphere become slowly but increasingly put into question.

AGENCY AND THE SPECTACLE

As we mentioned in the first chapter, a series of political events in the U.S. since the 1960s were starting to shape the field of political communication anew, giving life to new strands of research that valued the visual as a fundamental component of political life. One of the very first critical texts devoted to the intersection of politics and the visual in the U.S. could be considered Daniel Boorstin's 1962 seminal book *The Image: A Guide to Pseudo-Events in America*[61], where the author coined the term 'pseudo-event' in response to the increasing tendency

[61] D. J. BOORSTIN, *The Image: A Guide to Pseudo-Events in America* (New York: Harper, 1962).

of news and journalistic media to cover what he deemed to be 'unreal', 'unauthentic' happenings.

The term pseudo-event was born out of Boorstin's suggestion that, starting from the second half of the 20th century, political actors and media professionals tightened their relationship of mutual convenience: as politicians strived to satisfy the media's hunger for news, the latter was favorably maximizing their public exposure. In the pages of the book, Boorstin shares his concern towards the post-modernization of politics[62] and examines the symptoms of a revolutionary change in the field of political communication where "the image, more interesting than the original, has itself become the original", and where "the shadow has become the substance"[63].

The rise of pseudo-events is described by the author as a poisonous source for our experience, which offers a seemingly satisfying simulation of what politics is: the persuasive use of imagery during TV interviews, news releases, party rallies, and press conferences has spoiled citizens' "appetite for plain fact" and turned them into an invisible audience[64]. Needless to say,

---

[62] In their article "Postmodern Politics and the Battle for the Future," (1998), Steven Best and Douglas Kellner argue that the first form of postmodern politics began to take shape during the 1960s, influenced by events that occurred in France, the United States, and elsewhere, as well as by emerging postmodern theories. According to the authors, there is not one form of postmodern politics, but rather a whole set of conflicting positions that emerge from the diversity and ambiguities of the various postmodern theoretical perspectives (i.e. an affirmative postmodern politics, a nihilistic postmodern politics, and more). Some of the key insights of postmodern politics are the fragmentation of politics and political identities, the politicization of all spheres of social and personal existence, the shift from macropolitics to micropolitics and the radicalization of the theme of participatory democracy which is advocated in a variety of fields and domains of social life.

[63] D. J. BOORSTIN, *The Image: A Guide to Pseudo-Events in America* (New York: Harper, 1962), 204.

[64] IBID, 150.

Boorstin believed that pseudo-events were a disruptive force for the well-being of Western democracy – although probably inevitable.

In some way, Boorstin's insight seems to have anticipated Guy Debord's *Society of the Spectacle* by almost five years. However, as soon as the television medium entered European homes, Debord's book became a reference point for many scholars and intellectuals from the old continent, who have since then associated the term 'Spectacle' with the increasing mediatization of the political discourse and all aspects of public and private life. Unlike Boorstin, who focused only on the changes related to the fields of journalism and politics in the North American scenario, Debord's Spectacle referred to an all-encompassing critique of culture rooted in a Marxist's view of society. According to Debord and his comrades of the Situationist International (1957–1972), the Spectacle was not merely a collection of images, but rather a social relation among people mediated by images. Inspired by the events of May '68 in France, where students and workers rebelled jointly to overthrow the existing government, Debord's notion of the society of the Spectacle linked media with consumer society to warn about the commodification of politics to the detriment of the 'real' political life – deemed to be found off-screen and into the streets.

In the years following Debord's publication, the concept of the Spectacle had a major impact on a variety of modern theories of society and culture. In particular, one of the critiques by Debord that was most elaborated by scholars and intellectuals was the idea that, in a political culture dominated by media, individuals become passive subjects who contemplate a reified Spectacle. French sociologist Jean Baudrillard, for example, argued that the increased exposure of the political discourse to marketing-like communication techniques had turned citizens into *consumers* of politics instead of *producers* of it. In the transition from an industrial ("metallurgic") society to a symbolic ("semiurgic") one, Baudrillard saw politics increasingly conditioned to a new social order structured by models, codes, and signs[65]. As events or situations were replaced with virtual, electronic, or digitized images and signs, he argued that the real blurred into the unreal until simulation and reality collapsed onto each other becoming a hyperreality[66].

The work of Baudrillard explicitly draws from Walter Benjamin and Marshall McLuhan but, unlike them, he did not appear to foresee any empowerment or redemption of the masses. Instead, he described the latter as "an *in vacuo* aggregation of individual particles, refuse of the social and of media impulses: an opaque nebula whose growing density absorbs all the surrounding energy and light rays, to collapse finally under its own weight"[67]; according to Baudrillard, the mass was "a black hole which engulfs the social"[68].

Clearly, the reasoning behind Boorstin's and Baudrillard's works is concomitant with the rise of television – which shook the grounds of politics and political communication to an unimaginable extent. However, even before its widespread appearance in Western households, Theodor Adorno and Max Horkheimer had already foreseen television as a new tool of mass culture, and used it as an expedient to express their concept of the "culture industry". In *Dialectic of Enlightenment*, the authors refer to television as a prototypical artifact that would reduce culture to a series of industrialized, consumable goods by intensifying "the impoverishment of aesthetic matter" and

---

[65] J. BAUDRILLARD, *For a Critique of the Political Economy of the Sign* (Candor: Telos Press, 1981).

[66] J. BAUDRILLARD, *Simulacra and Simulation* (Ann Arbor: University of Michigan Press, 1994).

[67] J. BAUDRILLARD, *In the Shadow of the Silent Majorities: Or, The End of the Social and Other Essays* (Cambridge, MA: Semiotext(e), 1983), 3–4.

[68] BAUDRILLARD, *In the Shadow of the Silent Majorities*, 4.

thus "fulfilling the Wagnerian dream of the *Gesamtkunstwerk*, the fusion of all the arts in one work"[69].

Following the Frankfurt School's analyses, German philosopher Herbert Marcuse further added in his seminal book *One-Dimensional Man* that television could be considered as a legitimate apparatus of administration and domination, arguing that "with the control of information, with the absorption of individuals into mass communication, knowledge is administered and confined"[70]. Drawing from the lessons of Georg Lukács and Henri Lefebvre, the Spectacle was conceptualized by Boorstin, Baudrillard, Horkheimer, Adorno, Marcuse and many other major Frankfurt School theorists as a new device for consumer capitalism, where images supplanted real and active social participation in favor of alienation and social atomization.

When applied to politics, the Spectacle became a wide conceptual metaphor able to describe a one-to-one functional relationship between political actors and the media – which maximized each one's exposure but that ultimately excluded citizens from the democratic process and turned them into passive spectators harnessed by hyperrealities that forced their silence. However, while for most of the aforementioned authors media always appeared as a force to control, dominate and mislead people, Debord conceived the latter as a neutral set of devices that can change and adapt its functions in relation to the specific social and temporal relations in which it operates. This key concept, highlighted by Marco Briziarelli and Emiliana Armano in their book *The Spectacle 2.0: Reading Debord in the Context of Digital Capitalism*[71], is probably what left the Debordian

[69] M. HORKHEIMER AND T.W. ADORNO, *Dialectic of Enlightenment* (London: Allen Lane, 1973), 124.

[70] H. MARCUSE, *One Dimensional Man: Studies in the Ideology of Advanced Industrial Society* (Boston: Beacon Press, 1964), 104.

[71] M. BRIZIARELLI AND E. ARMANO, "Introduction: From the Notion of Spectacle to Spectacle 2.0: The Dialectic of Capitalist

concept of the Spectacle so open to future interpretations. One of the most compelling re-readings of Debord's Spectacle is undoubtedly that of critical theorists Steven Best and Douglas Kellner, who on the threshold of the new millennium questioned Debord in view of the emergence of the internet. In the article *Debord, Cybersituations, and the Interactive Spectacle*, Best and Kellner underline how new media paved the way for a new stage of the Spectacle: the "interactive Spectacle"[72]. "In the previous stage of the Spectacle", the authors argue, "the media and technology were seen as powerful control mechanisms keeping individuals numb, fragmented, and docile, watching and consuming, rather than acting and doing"[73]. However, the internet soon challenged this assumption, enabling "individuals to create and interact more productively with others in their everyday lives and to struggle to transform culture and society, generating new spaces of connection, freedom, and creativity"[74].

For example, the authors explain how the Zapatista guerrilla armies struggling in Chiapas, Mexico, were using computer databases as a medium to circulate their ideas via bulletins and mobilize individuals throughout the world to support their struggles against repressive state actions between 1994 and 1995[75]. Best and Kellner claim that the interactive Spectacle presents itself as highly ambiguous: on one side it calls for the creation of new cultural spaces and possibilities for the

---

Mediations," in *The Spectacle 2.0: Reading Debord in the Context of Digital Capitalism*, ed. Marco Briziarelli and Emiliana Armano (London: University of Westminster Press, 2017), 22.

[72] S. BEST AND D. KELLNER, "Debord, Cybersituations, and the Interactive Spectacle," *SubStance* 28, no. 3 (1999): 129–56.

[73] BEST AND KELLNER, "Debord, Cybersituations, and the Interactive Spectacle", 144.

[74] IBID, 150.

[75] IBID, 151.

empowerment of individuals and social groups, but on the other it implies new forms of seduction and domination.

Today, Briziarelli and Armano argue that Western societies find themselves in the most updated version of the Spectacle, dubbed as 'Spectacle 2.0'. According to the authors, the Spectacle 2.0 can be defined as a "historicized continuum"[76] of the Debordian one, but with one substantive difference: if Debord's Spectacle was a social relation between people mediated by images that are commodified through a vertical system of production, the internet and especially social networking service (SNS) allows a new system of image-production and, by implication, new forms of relation between people.

Whilst the original conceptualization of the Spectacle represented the spectator as a passive receptor of the Spectacle's agency and a victim of crude manipulation, the spectator of the Spectacle 2.0 is an interactive subject "who socializes through language tools and flexible digital technology, characterized much more ambiguously by initiative, creativity, exploitation and precariousness"[77].

In *The Spectacle 2.0: Reading Debord in the Context of Digital Capitalism*, Briziarelli and Armano critically inquire how informational capitalism modified the ways in which knowledge workers produce, consume and reproduce value, highlighting the new forms of precarious (digital) labor emerging from it. In the Spectacle 2.0, human social lives are both the mediated objects and the mediating subjects: subjectivities are themselves the products of the Spectacle[78].

[76] ARMANO AND BRIZIARELLI, *The Spectacle 2.0*, 34.

[77] IBID, 34.

[78] C. BASSETTI, A. MURGIA, AND M. TELI, "Tin Hat Games – Producing, Funding, and Consuming an Independent Role-Playing Game in the Age of the Interactive Spectacle," in *The Spectacle 2.0*, ed. Marco Briziarelli and Emiliana Armano (London: University of Westminster Press, 2017), 167–82.

Within the field of political communication, the Spectacle 2.0 has brought a true revolution by changing or subverting the spaces, subjects, and modes of interaction that were in use before the advent of the internet. Firstly, the massive use of SNS by political actors and parties has partially reallocated the political activity from physical spaces to virtual ones, causing a significant expansion and globalization of the political arena and thus also of political discourse; secondly, this new and broader environment has allowed for the flowering of new figures (both professional and amateur) shaping the political discourse; lastly, all of these actors performing in the Spectacle 2.0 (politicians, professionals, amateurs) have access to a wide array of digital tools to deliver campaign messages, ads, commentaries, satire, and any other form of political communication which are at the same time fostered and constrained by the medium's logic(s).

In short, if traditional media were based on a vertical model of information transmission, the system inherent to new media seems to foster a more horizontal one. In this new political landscape, the main communication actors are not just journalists, politicians and communication designers who supervise the creation of political content, but also citizen-users who are giving life to a new, decentralized, and *apparently* disintermediated form of political communication.

This shift in the conceptualization of the Spectacle seems to have been widely embraced by designers, who in the last thirty years have become increasingly aware of their capacity to tackle political and social challenges and have given life to a whole new range of artifacts and theories. However, since the advent of the internet, designers have struggled to face the issue of visual representation in a system where the Spectacle seems to dominate the majority of the communication strategies adopted in the political discourse.

In particular, I argue that the most significant challenges that designers are facing since the onset of the Spectacle 2.0 could be linked to three main factors or causes. Firstly, that the Spectacle 2.0 has led to the progressive dissolution of physical spaces for the political and democratic exercise in favor of digitally mediated ones, partially destabilizing the practice of design. Secondly, that the Spectacle 2.0 has led to a state of permanent electoral campaign which challenged the role of designers within the 'voting system' and pushed them towards the increasing use of design as a means to challenge and put into question political practices and politics itself. And lastly, that the Spectacle 2.0 has established new hegemonic agendas of global development and neoliberal capitalization, urging designers to re-imagine the very idea of neo-liberal politics into new counter-hegemonic political systems.

Ultimately, it seems that the confrontation between design and this hyper-spectacularized political system calls for a new design vision, or at least a redefinition of its practice. And this is probably why, starting in the 1990s, so many design critics, theorists and practitioners started to develop a whole new range of theories, methodologies and approaches that increasingly put to question the agency of design within the political field.

Not surprisingly, one of the most discussed topics in the last three decades concerns the increasing erosion of design's agency in parallel with the emergence of new places and spaces for political action – a shift strongly marked by the beginning of the new millennium. In fact, starting from the 21st century, the collision between the political sphere and the Information Age generated a series of transformations which relentlessly changed the ways citizens experience democracy, both in terms of space and time[79].

Whilst the Western pre-Information Age's political space corresponded often to an identifiable, tangible and sociable

---

[79] J. MEYROWITZ, *No Sense of Place: The Impact of Electronic Media on Social Behavior* (Oxford University Press, 1986), 308.

dimensionality, the contemporary space of and for politics is moving towards an ever changing, more slippery ground. Clearly, this shift did not result from one unequivocal event, but rather over the course of many years and at pace with technological development, where citizens and politicians went from pursuing their political activity first in designated places and later in 'non-supervised' spaces. They went from living democracy in 'explicit' venues consisting of floors, walls and ceilings, to 'implicit' venues, places not necessarily thought for politics and maybe not even accordingly policy-equipped – like social networking sites.

The growing absence of public spaces and the constraining algorithmic forces dictated by SNS have forced the practice of design to find new spaces for its political action, which has increasingly shifted to places with a wider margin of scope. Two of these have undoubtedly been the spaces of fiction and criticism, which over the past three decades have proven to be instruments of (non-)action capable of altering the perception of the state of things. Fiction and criticism have developed as mechanisms of intervention capable of translating, changing or reading what is seen or experienced, and this is why they have proved particularly crucial in light of new conceptual categories such as the recent 'post-truth'.

As design researcher Sofia Gonçalves points out, in the face of an increasingly compromised and unsustainable information system, fiction "gives us permission to comment, to scrutinize, to underline the contradictions of reality, to reveal uncomfortable truths, without the responsibility of the factual; to create alternate realities that allow us to understand the world we have, that we will have in the future, that we aspire to have, or that we refuse"[80].

---

[80] S. GONÇALVES, "Vacant Lots and Insurmountable Territories: Communication Design between Reality and Fiction, between Expansion and Degrowth," in *Image in the Post-Millennium:*

In this sense, the imaginative capacity of fiction has allowed designers to find, in addition to a free space where it is possible to start 'anew,' a form of praxeology which, as *Fiction as Method* authors Jon K. Shaw and Theo Reeves-Evison point out, "can be used as [a] means of revealing the hidden workings of a state of affairs, and even of establishing a certain agency with it"[81].

Similarly, speculative and critical design (SCD) has increasingly become a tool used by designers to understand how to shift toward more desirable futures. According to the latest theoretical development by British designers Anthony Dunne and Fiona Raby, SCD often starts from insightful analyses on individuals' everyday interaction with objects and technology in order to provoke critical reflections from the observer or user. In their seminal book *Speculative Everything: Design, Fiction, and Social Dreaming*, the designers explain that "critical design is critical thinking translated into materiality," and is thus conceived as the action of thinking through design to question the assumptions of design itself, the limitations of the technology industry and its byproducts, and social and political theories in general[82].

Unlike fiction, SCD involves a materiality-oriented approach and line of thinking which often aims at triggering reflections on a given environment instead of inviting the viewer to observe an alternative reality. By challenging pre-established ideas, both in the designer and in the viewer, critical design works in the unstable and cloudy territory represented by the intersection of design, politics and culture, leading the maker and the viewer to meditate on their actions. In the past two decades, both design

Mediation, Process and Critical Tension, ed. Maria Joao Baltazar and Tomé Saldanha Quadros (Eindhoven: ONOMATOPEE, 2021), 37.

[81] JON K. SHAW AND THEO REEVES-EVISON, EDS., *Fiction as Method* (Cambridge, MA: Sternberg Press, 2017), 7.

[82] A. DUNNE AND F. RABY, *Speculative Everything: Design, Fiction, and Social Dreaming* (Cambridge, MA: MIT Press, 2013), 35.

fiction and SCD have proven to be key tools for navigating the uncertain social and political landscape that has characterized the 21st century. And yet, in both cases, these spaces seem often to refrain from a 'real' application to the lived world – thus limiting their scope for action and permanence.

Another challenge that designers appear to be facing since the onset of the Spectacle 2.0 is linked to the state of permanent electoral campaigning in which today's politics is immersed, coupled with an ever-expanding process of politics' aestheticization. Under such circumstances, in fact, many design practitioners seem to have pulled themselves out of the 'voting system' by approaching design as a means to rather challenge and put into question political practices and even politics itself.

In this respect, an interesting approach is that proposed by Carl DiSalvo in his concept of 'adversarial design', a practice that uses the means and forms of design to challenge beliefs, values, and what is taken to be fact. The author's use of the term 'adversary' draws heavily from political theorist Chantal Mouffe's formulation[83] of the political as a state of conflict and based on a relationship that includes disagreement and strife but that lacks a violent desire to abolish the other[84]. In the eponymous book[85], DiSalvo lifts the term adversary from its strictly political meaning and uses it to describe the character of designed artifacts or systems which operate in an 'agonistic' sense – that is, projects that are able to create 'battlefields' where citizens can rediscover

[83] Mouffe's theory of agonism reprises Carl Schmitt's (1996) formulation of the political as the identification between friends and enemies characterized by inherent conflict, but calls for the transformation of this antagonistic relation into an agonistic one between adversaries.

[84] C. MOUFFE, *The Return of the Political* (London: Verso, 2005); C. MOUFFE, *The Democratic Paradox* (London: Verso, 2000); C. MOUFFE, *Agonistics: Thinking The World Politically* (London: Verso, 2013).

[85] C. DISALVO, *Adversarial Design* (Cambridge, MA: MIT Press, 2015).

the right to disagree, to mobilize, and to collectively create alternatives to the current state of things.

Beyond the straightforward application of design to politics – like redesigning ballots and polling places as an attempt to improve governance – design is regarded as a contextual practice which strives to question conventional approaches to political issues. In today's polarized political visual culture, dominated by the populist imperative 'us versus them' and an increasingly aestheticized political discourse, DiSalvo's insight proves to be essential and necessary to restore a healthy and dialogical political confrontation – not determined solely by the interests of the political class. As Chantal Mouffe herself writes,

> "In our post-Fordist condition, at a time when design is widely used by capital to reproduce its hegemony, it is urgent to realize that design could also play a crucial role in counter-hegemonic politics. By shifting the way questions are posed, experiments in agonistic design bring to the fore issues that the hegemonic neo-liberal consensus tends to obscure and obliterate, and encourage the construction of new subjectivities"[86].

The point highlighted by Mouffe leads us to the last consideration of this section, which is that the Spectacle's hegemonic nature has survived and can still be seen in the Spectacle 2.0's power to manufacture consent through the effective promotion and establishment of a neoliberal ideology. As Debord argued in his 1988 follow-up book *Comments on the Society of the Spectacle*, the integrated Spectacle's truth (or hegemonic discourse) operates within neoliberalism and in accordance with

[86] C. MOUFFE, "Agonism, Democracy and Design," in Designing Everyday Life, ed. Jan Boelen and Vera Sacchetti (Zürich: Park Books, 2015), 48.

the interests of those who most benefit from it. For Debord, the integrated Spectacle succeeds as a hegemonic system because it has the ability to fragment both human consciousness and society, both of which can be successively re-integrated thanks to the mediating and articulating power of the Spectacle. Consent emerges therefore from an established regime of truth and from policies put into practice to fulfill the Spectacle's self-perpetuating cycle.

In the context of the Spectacle 2.0, where information and communication technologies have become pervasive tools that shape one's daily political activity (or non-activity), and at the same time the symbol of current form of labor exploitation, power structures and ideological (and counter-ideological) practices, design *could* and *should* be seen as a tool to re-imagine the very idea of neo-liberal politics into new counter-hegemonic political systems.

Although this goal seems very difficult to achieve, according to design theorist and philosopher Tony Fry, design owns both the capacity to understand the historical nature of the neo-liberal political unsustainability and the ability to change its future course. In his 1999 book *A New Design Philosophy: An Introduction to Defuturing*, Fry coined the term 'defuturing' precisely to describe – or better re*write* – the agency of design, charging designers with the ability to gain an understanding of the *historical* nature of the unsustainable (in ecological, social, and political terms) and identify the processes that are destroying common futures. However, as Fry aptly notes, "we need to remind ourselves that the future is never empty, never a blank space to be filled with the output of human activity. It is already colonized by what the past and present have sent to it"[87]. Without this comprehension, without an understanding

---

[87] T. FRY, *A New Design Philosophy: An Introduction to Defuturing* (Sydney: UNSW Press, 1999), 11–12.

of *how*, *when* and *why* the future has already been colonized by the ideas sent to it by the past, design' propensity will always be that to fulfill the wishes of the present with little attention to future needs. Building on Hannah Arendt's argument that "plurality is the law of the earth" and a *conditio per quam* of all political life[88], Fry proposes to transform design into "a huge politico-ethical meta-project that centers on establishing a 'common good' able to embrace the commonality of needs of humans and non-humans as a 'commonality in difference'"[89]. Since only the notion of plurality can help articulate relationships and exercise the practices of disjunction and association, a design artifact should be able to highlight precisely the diversity of the political spectrum and its contradictions.

According to Fry, the aim of design is not to be a 'service' – which is both inadequate and politically problematic. "What is actually needed first", says Fry in the preface of the 2020 edition of *Defuturing: A New Design Philosophy*, "is a new epistemological foundation for design" as well as the recognition of design *as* politics – both "as a servant of the defuturing status quo, and its positive form as the beginning of its remaking as a futuring agent of change"[90].

RE-IMAGINING MEDIATION

What do the pre-election debate of John Kennedy and Richard Nixon, the Watergate hearings in the U.S. Congress, the royal wedding of Charles and Diana, and the fall of the Berlin Wall have in common? According to the social scientists Daniel

[88] H. ARENDT, *The Life of the Mind* (New York: Harcourt, Brace & Co., 1978).

[89] T. FRY, *Design as Politics* (London: Bloomsbury, 2010), 99.

[90] T. FRY, *Defuturing: A New Design Philosophy* (London: Bloomsbury Visual Arts, 2020), XXVI.

Dayan and Elihu Katz, they can all be considered *media events*. In 1992, the two authors popularized[91] this term in media research through their seminal book *Media Events: The Live Broadcasting of History*[92] to denote a radical shift that was taking place in popular culture after the progressive introduction of television in western homes. In the book, Dayan and Katz describe a series of preplanned historical events (such as those mentioned above) and analyze how their intrinsic aesthetic, performative, and entertaining qualities were shaping new forms of political participation and involvement. Inspired by the work of Émile Durkheim, Claude Lévi-Strauss, and Victor Turner, Dayan and Katz argued that the live broadcast of preplanned ceremonial events on television was able to bring citizens together in a common viewing experience, transporting them to "the sacred center of the society"[93].

Dayan and Katz believed that the experience of media events was different from the experience of everyday television, as it allowed viewers to assume a ceremonial role and create a 'sense of occasion'. The authors claim indeed that media events are "reminiscent of holy days", both because of the simultaneous and common participation to the event and because of the "liturgical" staging and experiencing of it[94].

Albeit written in a period of absolute television-predominance, the work of Dayan and Katz was published among a general,

---

[91] The term 'media event', as well as other theories and concepts contained in the book, had already been developed by the authors in their previous works (cf. in particular to KATZ, 1988; KATZ ET AL., 1981; KATZ & DAYAN, 1985, 1986).

[92] D. DAYAN AND E. KATZ, *Media Events: The Live Broadcasting of History* (Cambridge, MA: Harvard University Press, 1992).

[93] E. SHILS, *Center and Periphery: Essays in Macrosociology* (Chicago: University of Chicago Press, 1975).

[94] D. DAYAN AND E. KATZ, *Media Events: The Live Broadcasting of History* (Cambridge, MA: Harvard University Press, 1992), 16.

deep-seated academic skepticism towards this medium. In the preface of the book, the authors even defend themselves from critics by stating that, even if they "worry – intermittently – about becoming apostles of a telecommunications genre that invites politicians to perform on the stage of the world", and although they take the lesson of Daniel Boorstin very seriously, they "refuse to [...] reecho the warning that the 'aestheticization of politics' can take only one political direction"[95]. In this sense, the book by Dayan and Katz can be read as an attempt to rectify intellectuals' disdain for television by challenging scholars in the social sciences to bring the unbiased study of television into political analysis – focusing on the extraordinary and singular aspects that this medium could play in everyday life with an anthropological eye rather than relying solely on quantitative data.

In addition to demonstrating the effects of television and having contributed to debunk the academic skepticism towards this medium, the work of Dayan and Katz provided major contributions to the fields of media studies, social sciences, and political theory in many aspects. Most significantly, *Media Events* contributed to the spread of the concept of disintermediation, which had already been introduced by Katz a few years earlier in his influential article *Disintermediation: Cutting Out the Middle Man*[96].

In the book, Dayan and Katz define disintermediation as "the process whereby media events allow their principals to talk over the heads of the middlemen who normally mediate between leaders and their public"[97]. Specifically, the authors define the model of disintermediation as a one-step communication process (A → C) that surpasses the classic two-step one (A → B →

[95] DAYAN AND KATZ, *Media Events*, VII.
[96] E. KATZ, "Disintermediation: Cutting Out the Middle Man," *Intermedia* 16, NO. 2 (March 1988): 30–31.
[97] DAYAN AND KATZ, *Media Events*, 214.

C), where one or more actors (A) – whether from religious, sport or political backgrounds – have the power to cut the middleman (B) out of the communication process and reach a public (C) by means of a new medium (D)[98]. Towards the end of their reasoning, Dayan and Katz conclude that "the introduction of a new medium may transform not only a 'message', not only the nature of response, but an entire structure of social relations", thus redefining "the relative power of organizers, intermediaries, broadcasters, and viewers"[99] (FIG. 34).

After new media integrated into the media matrix, most of the images shaping the Western political discourse do not come from television anymore, and the way that public figures speak with the public (and vice versa) has profoundly changed. In particular, SNS have caused a radical shift in political communication standards, implementing new tools for the creation and dissemination of political messages and expanding the range of players who have access to these tools. For these and many other reasons, this renewed media reality has brought the attention of scholars from different fields back on the notion of media events, which has been redefined and extended to fit the current phase of "postmodern campaigning"[100].

---

[98] For example, the authors recall the fireside chats given by Franklin Roosevelt (A), who by means of the new medium of radio (D) spoke directly to the American people (C) over the heads of the Congress (B). (Dayan & Katz, 1992, p. 215)

[99] IBID, 217.

[100] In Norris's words: "Post-modern campaigns are understood as those where the coterie of professional consultants on advertising, public opinion, marketing, and strategic news management become more co-equal actors with politicians, assuming a more influential role within government in a 'permanent' campaign, as well as coordinating local activity more tightly at the grassroots. The news media fragments into a more complex and incoherent environment of multiple channels, outlets, and levels. And the electorate becomes more dealigned in their voting choices. For some citizens, the election may represent a return to

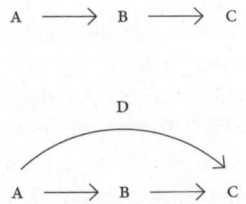

FIG. 34
Disintermediation process (A = principal, B = traditional intermediaries, C = public, D = new medium). Elaboration from the original figure in Dayan and Katz (1994, p. 215).

In the contemporary political context, SNS have extended the opportunity – for citizens and politicians alike – to autonomously generate and spread media events online, extending the capacity of disintermediation to an unprecedented level. On one hand, Western political actors have adopted an increasingly wide array of internet-based communication tools, giving rise to new visual strategies, hiring new professionals, and trying to capitalize votes through the opportunities offered by SNS. On the other, SNS themselves have opened up a new scenario where online users have become political communication's amateurs, wandering in a digital world where their actions are characterized by an ever-greater visibility.

Of course, SNS have not monopolized the field of political communication; the Western political discourse unravels both through traditional media such as newspapers, radio shows, and television news programs and new media such as websites, blogs, and digital apps. However, platforms such as Facebook, YouTube, Twitter and Instagram have assumed an increasingly pivotal role in the Western political landscape due to their easy access and wide reach. And since new media allow political actors to relay information directly to individuals without the

some of the forms of engagement found in the pre-modern stage, as the new channels of communication potentially allow greater interactivity between voters and politicians". From: P. NORRIS, "The Evolution of Election Campaigns: Eroding Political Engagement?," in *Conference on Political Communications in the 21st. Century* (St Margaret's College, University of Otago, New Zealand, 2004), 3.

intervention of any gatekeeper, they are often preferred compared to traditional media – which lack immediacy and do not allow control over the message or its distribution.

One of the many effects of the increasing use of SNS in political discourse has been to give rise to an alleged 'unmediated' or 'unfiltered' kind of communication. This idea has been often put forward by populist leaders and parties, who in recent years have accused the western media system of being controlled by 'intellectual élites' who represent the enemy of 'the people'. Building on this assumption, populist political actors often praise SNS as the only neutral and independent arena for political discourse because it allows them to communicate directly with their electorate, advocate unrestricted popular sovereignty and reinforce the image of a friendly approachability. But can political discourse on SNS be *really* disintermediated?

Whether it is political actors or citizens who make use of them, SNS present an ambivalent and contradictory situation. Their presence in the western political discourse has redefined the rules and boundaries of journalism, displaced intermediaries, and affected the organizational forms of politics itself – thus questioning *who* are the gatekeepers in today's political landscape. But in spite of that, communications occurring on SNS are anything but free from intermediaries. Rather, there are new intermediaries which mediate between political actors and users – primarily the algorithms that govern SNS, which in turn give origin to a series of biases to which the message is subjected from its generated form to its read one. Therefore, even if some political actors sell their kind of communication as 'unmediated' and 'unfiltered', political messages on SNS are actually the result of an ultra-mediated communication framework, where the flood of information sees the message manipulated and partialized by both algorithmic forces and biases.

In the field of design, the 1990s and early 2000s witnessed an emerging concern over a series of processes conveniently gathered under the umbrella term of 'mediation' – which broadly indicates the study of the phenomena occurring between the production and consumption of artifacts.

On the one hand, the issue of mediation resulted in a greater awareness on the role of mediating discourses in generating meanings for designed goods and processes. On the other, it led to the conceptualization of new analytical frameworks which aimed at understanding the roles that technologies play in mediating design activities.

In fact, as the philosopher of technology Peter-Paul Verbeek wrote in his article *Materializing Morality: Design Ethics and Technological Mediation*, "technological artifacts are not neutral intermediaries", but rather "actively co-shape people's being in the world: their perceptions and actions, experience, and existence"[101] (FIG. 35).

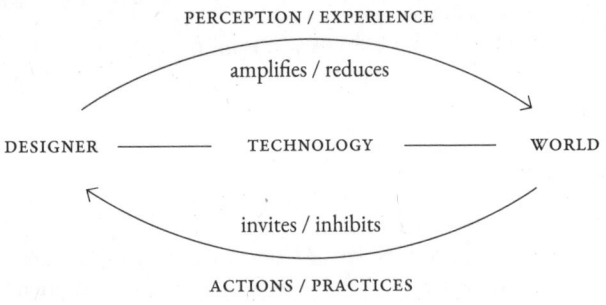

FIG. 35
Influences between the human and the world in Verbeek's technological mediation theory. Elaboration from the original figure in HAUSER, S., OOGJES, D., WAKKARY, R., & VERBEEK, P.-P. (2018). *An Annotated Portfolio on Doing Postphenomenology Through Research Products*: 466.

101 P-P. VERBEEK, "Materializing Morality: Design Ethics and Technological Mediation," *Science, Technology, & Human Values* 31, NO. 3 (May 2006): 364.

Drawing from the work of science philosopher Don Ihde, Verbeek developed the theory of technological mediation as a framework to read and analyze the roles technologies play in human existence and in society. This mediation approach, however, "urges us to give up the idea that we are autonomous and sovereign beings, who have authority over technology and its implications"[102]. The conception of a technologically mediated being, says Verbeek, is hard to digest due to our image of the self as an autonomous subject – an idea deeply rooted in the post-Enlightenment modernist metaphysics that discerns the human (who possesses intentionality and freedom) from the object (seen instead as an instrument forged and governed by human intentions).

Applied to the field of design, the mediation theory proposed by Verbeek sees designers 'released' from their role as gatekeepers, since "The mediating role of technologies is *not only* the result of the activities of the designers, who inscribe scripts[103] or delegate responsibilities, but also depends on *users*, who interpret and appropriate technologies, and on the *technologies themselves*, which can evoke emergent forms of mediation"[104] (FIG. 36).

[102] IBID, 171.

[103] The word 'script' in the Verbeek quote refers to a concept developed by Madeleine Akrich and Bruno Latour in the early 1990s to describe the manifold roles technological artifacts play in different contexts of use. According to the authors, the script is the product of the "inscription" or "delegation" of functions by designers on a specific artifact, a sort of "user manual" which assigns specific responsibilities to the artifact and anticipates how users will interact with it. Instead, de-scription, write Akrich and Latour, "is possible only if some extraordinary event – a crisis – modifies the direction of the translation from things back to words and allows the analyst to trace the movement from words to things".
M. AKRICH AND B. LATOUR "A Summary of a Convenient Vocabulary for the Semiotics of Human and Nonhuman Assemblies." In *Shaping Technology/ Building Society. Studies in Sociotecnical Change*, edited by W.E. Bijker and J. Law, 259–64. Cambridge, MA: MIT Press, 1992.

[104] IBID, 372 (emphasis added).

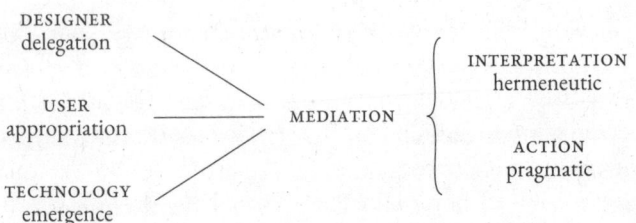

FIG. 36
Multifold roles present in Verbeek's technological mediation theory. Elaboration from the original figure in Verbeek (2006, p. 372).

Acknowledging Verbeek's technological mediation in the design field means enabling an interaction with the agency of future users, technology and the unpredictability of their mediating roles. However, this stance challenges many assumptions on the practice of design and the role of designers themselves. As put beautifully into question by British anthropologist Tim Ingold:

> "How can designers move from devising solutions that constrain practitioners to play by their own rules, to a position in which these rules are open to negotiation, and in which the improvisatory interventions of practitioners present an opportunity rather than a threat? How can designers avoid falling into the Panglossian fallacy of a 'user-centered' design which still treats practitioners as the mere consumer of objects that are ready-made for them and perfectly suited to their needs, rather than as designers and makers in their own rights?"[105]

[105] T. INGOLD, "Introduction: The Perception of the User-Producer," in *Design and Anthropology*, ed. Wendy Gunn and Jared Donovan, Anthropological Studies on Creativity and Perception (Farnham: Ashgate Publishing, 2012), 32.

To reformulate the idea of design so radically implies not only a fundamental refashioning of the role of the designer, but also a new form of attention towards the intersecting spheres of production and consumption. In a field where consumption has been traditionally considered "as a passive function in which the consumer conforms and adapts to directives issued by the producer"[106], the introduction of a thought pattern which attributes greater competencies to the consumer or user as well as to technology itself represents a major breakthrough. This has prompted a growing interest in mediation from design scholars in the fields of design history and design culture who have engaged in critical debates on the practices and processes regarding mediating activities such as the organization, exposition and communication of design itself.

On this subject, a great example is provided by design historian Grace Lees-Maffei in her 2009 contribution to the Journal of Design History, where she evolved the Production-Consumption model[107] elaborated by J. A. Walker into a Production-Consumption-Mediation one. The PCM paradigm within design history can be associated with a general shift from the object as the unit of study to a broader analysis of the cultural meanings of artifacts which, by looking at the phenomena occurring between production and consumption, could provide fundamental insights into understanding artifacts' cultural significance. In fact, the paradigm introduced by

---

[106] K. FALLAN, "De-Scribing Design: Appropriating Script Analysis to Design History," *Design Issues* 24, NO. 4 (October 2008): 67.

[107] In his book *Design History and the History of Design* (1990), John A. Walker illustrated the Production-Consumption Model to illustrate the functioning of the industrial manufacturing system, explaining how design has been framed and exercised from the Industrial Revolution onwards. Although Walker himself stated it to be necessarily incomplete, the model has been widely used by many design scholars as a basis for the analysis of design practices.

Lees-Maffei aims at providing new perspectives on the issues of production and consumption "not through the examination of designers' intentions or actual consumption practices, but rather through the analysis of the cultural and social significance of designed objects, spaces, and processes"[108].

Lees-Maffei claims that the mediation focus "enables recognition of the fact that design is much more than the object; it is a complex web of surrounding practices and discourses"[109]. Specifically, according to the author, three mutually constitutive phenomena shape the socio-cultural significance of design. Firstly, the role played by "channels such as television, magazines, corporate literature, advice literature and so on in mediating between producers and consumers," which contribute to "forming consumption practices and ideas about design". Secondly, the acknowledgment of the importance of mediating channels, which are "themselves designed and therefore open to design historical analysis". And thirdly "the role of designed goods themselves as mediating devices", as they "mediate between producer and consumer, just as they are used to mediate relations between individuals"[110].

The intuitions by Lees-Maffei and Verbeek are part of a larger series of observations gathered in the aftermath of the internet's arrival regarding the space that design occupies in mediating processes. The general recognition that mediation occurs both in the practice of design and in the processes by which design is produced and consumed is critical in order to rewrite a new conception of design that re-centers the practice within an increasingly complex and changing technological scenario. With the progressive dissolution of the line between production and consumption, design has started to be no longer conceived as

[108] G. LEES-MAFFEI, "The Production–Consumption–Mediation Paradigm," *Journal of Design History* 22, NO. 4 (December 1, 2009): 366.
[109] IBID, 372.
[110] IBID, 366.

the mere construction of graphics, products, services, and environments, but rather as a means to explore the visible and invisible. Instead of presenting themselves as 'transmitters' of information, in the contemporary (digital) communication media, system designers turn into both producers and interpreters of the given media environment in which they operate.

Today, the questions that designers pose to contemporary society are frequently questions directed at themselves, framed in meta-projects that depict the hyper-mediate landscape within which political processes take place, but that also reflect on their own (in)ability to provide answers. Since it both forges and depends on cultural, social, and technological constraints to bring systems and artifacts into the world, design is now more than ever a tool to frame questions about visual culture and image production and represent them symbolically – especially those regarding the creation of political meaning.

THE ISSUE OF AUTHORSHIP

Starting from the mid 1990s, an increasing number of scholars have concentrated their studies on the process of the *personalization* of politics. The causes behind this process are numerous, and they vary depending on a country's general population, electoral system, access to media, as well as the contingent events that shape one country's political history. Nevertheless, one could broadly define the personalization of politics in Western countries as the result of the changes occurring in the reciprocal relationship between media, parties, and citizens – and thus as the junction among three forms of personalization.

The first form of personalisation concerns a shift in media focus from the politician as occupier of a public role to the politician as a private individual. Following the thesis of American political scientist W. Lance Bennett, the roots of this form of personalization can be traced broadly to the social changes starting from the early 1970s, which collided with the diffusion of a neoliberal trade regime able to transform global production, finance, labor, and consumption patterns[111]. During this historic period, Bennet argues, the ideals and practices of neoliberal economics became so pervasive that they were able to drive the social and economic 'traditional' equality values of parties to the political margin, thus shifting their stances towards hybrid models of bipartisanism. The consequent partisan dealignment in most Western democracies caused a progressive dissolution of partisan loyalship, first consisting of a strong social bond between the citizen and a specific party. In these circumstances, weaker voter attachment to parties made voters more likely to rely on the appeal of the candidate's personality in order to decide their vote.

A further change in the political context that influences the role of leaders in the electoral choice is the decline of electoral participation. The assumption is that declining turnout enhances the role of the president or the prime minister, by focusing greater attention on the leader's role in mobilizing the vote, above and beyond party considerations. In addition, the decline in electoral participation produces voters who might be more motivated by economic self-interest in reaching their voting decision.

In such a context, the role of the leader in framing and promoting policies to attract these voters has proved to become more important over the course of time[112]. The desire of voters to hold governments accountable for their actions provides a

---

[111] W. L. BENNETT, "The Personalization of Politics: Political Identity, Social Media, and Changing Patterns of Participation," *The Annals of the American Academy of Political and Social Science* 644 (2012): 20–39, 24.

[112] I. MCALLISTER, "The Personalization of Politics," in The Oxford Handbook of Political Behavior, ed. Russell J. Dalton and Hans-Dieter Klingemann (Oxford: Oxford University Press, 2007), 571–88.

further explanation for the emphasis on the personalities of the leaders, who clearly have a stronger appeal if compared to an abstract institution or a political ideal[113]. This tendency is ever more important in parliamentary systems, where the responsibility of collective cabinets and the fortunes of the government as a whole may blur accountability in the eyes of the public. By focusing attention on the prime minister as the individual who is accountable for the government's collective performance, the public finds it easier to deliver reward or punishment if compared to an abstract collectivity. As a result, there is a general trend towards a stronger correlation overtime between prime ministerial popularity and the public's increasingly poor rating of governments[114].

These changes in the partisan and electoral context have several important consequences for the personalization of politics. Firstly, political leaders are now important not just for voter conversion, but for mobilization as well – traditionally the major function of political parties – to the extent that voters respond either positively or negatively according to their personalities. Secondly, leaders now hold their positions by virtue of a personalized mandate rather than because of a support base within the party, meaning that leaders can appeal to voters over the heads of the party and often bypass party factions. And lastly, once a leader is popularly elected, the personalized mandate that he or she possesses will convey considerable policy

---

[113] C. BEAN AND A. MUGHAN, "Leadership Effects in Parliamentary Elections in Australia and Britain," *American Political Science Review* 83, NO. 4 (December 1989): 1165–79.

[114] D. J. LANOUE AND B. HEADRICK, "Prime Ministers, Parties, and the Public: The Dynamics of Government Popularity in Great Britain," *The Public Opinion Quarterly* 58, NO. 2 (1994): 191–209; I. MCALLISTER, "Prime Ministers, Opposition Leaders and Government Popularity in Australia," *Australian Journal of Political Science* 38, NO. 2 (July 2003): 259–77.

autonomy, with little or no recourse to the party to which the leader belongs.

The second form of personalization traces back to the growth of the electronic media, and especially television, during the 1950s and 1960s. In the early years of the development of television, relatively few resources were devoted to the coverage of politics, which was not considered suited to the new medium[115]. However, that view changed rapidly as the potential of television to market politics to voters became widely apparent for several reasons. The most obvious is that television favors the representation of the leader's body, which can attract the attention of viewers more than an abstract account of political happenings and makes it easier for viewers to develop a relationship with the politicians and to empathize with their goals. Viewers may place themselves in the role of the candidates they see on television, or in the role of the interviewers who interrogate them, and as a consequence gain a better understanding of the politician's views. For television, political leaders represent a convenient visual shortcut to capture and retain the viewer's attention, particularly if the information overlaps with the leader's personality.

In today's political scenario, this form of personalization has reached critical levels due to the increasing implementation of SNS in the political discourse – both by political actors and citizens. If television had proved to be an efficient consensus-generating mechanism for political actors, SNS are now able to capture users' behavior on the internet through a collection of data (such as the user's location, language spoken, biographical data, shared links, and/or tracking cookies) generated through the user's interactions within a specific platform. SNS can help politicians to tailor messages by creating different content according to the data collected by the party on a specific platform

---

[115] T. E. PATTERSON, *Out of Order* (New York: Vintage Books, 1994).

and delivering them through the use of the platform's algorithm – thus giving rise to an increasingly personalized political experience.

The last form of personalization involves the citizen-user which, as mentioned earlier, gained more recognition as a player in this political landscape dominated by new media. As I have shown in the first chapter, the identity politics of the social movements that developed around the 1960s centered mostly either on group identity (women, minorities, etc.) or cause issues (the war in Vietnam, anti-Gaullism, etc). However, these 'older' forms of political inclusion today merge together and give rise to new conditions for the formation of political participation, which according to scholars W. Lance Bennett and Alexandra Segerberg[116] can be considered as a combination of an inclusiveness defined by tolerance for different viewpoints, the rise of crowd-sourced inclusive personal action frames that lower the barriers to identification (i.e. "We are the 99%"), and the pervasive use of SNS, which allows individuals to share their own stories and concerns and become important catalysts of collective action.

What emerges from these conditions is that, in today's political landscape, SNS allow public manifestations of expression that pave the way for new forms of civic engagement. These include subversive movements and organizations on social media (e.g. Occupy Wall Street, the Arab Spring, etc.), political commentaries (i.e. meme or satirical social media pages), and political supporters of one specific party or candidate (political fandom). Furthermore, the greater access to authoring and editing tools provided by new media sees a growing multitude of actors contributing to the production of political content. On one hand there are political actors, whose bodies and faces

---

[116] BENNETT AND SEGERBERG, "Digital Media and the Personalization of Collective Action."

have become central figures in the representation of politics and who have hired new professional figures to supervise the creation of visual political content on different media platforms. On the other hand there are citizen-users, who are giving life to new forms of DIY political content which have enabled prosumers to rail against the prescribed design '*dicta*' and more 'traditional' forms of political representation.

Lastly, there are new media themselves, and in particular SNS, which are revolutionizing all stages of political communication and are transforming the property of images into something created, edited, and monitored by an ever-expanding public but ultimately owned by everyone and no one at the same time. As the *loci* of political content production are distributed across disparate authorial selves, it is legitimate to ask whether there is any room left for designers contributing to the Western political discourse, and what their position within it is.

The issue regarding the position of designers with respect to political issues fits into a wider debate within design studies which dates back to the beginning of the 1980s, where practitioners, educators and scholars began to question their practice in relation to technological developments. This process of questioning coincides with many experiences occurring simultaneously across Western countries which, as a whole, has cast doubt on the modernist conventions of professional design – now subjected to deliberate interrogation.

From the typographic work of Weingard to the experience at the Cranbrook Academy of Art under the lead of Katherine McCoy, designers have long addressed the age-old issue of authorship, trying to figure out how to negotiate their position and offer more interpretative space to the reader. In particular, throughout the 1990s, many designers began to question their role within their own practice as well as in society more in general, adopting a post-structuralist (re)reading of their work.

In these years, one of the texts on this topic that proved to be most significant was Michael Rock's famous essay *Designer as Author*, published in 1996 in Eye magazine, where the American graphic designer examined the notion of the author in the field of graphic design. By reviving classic discourses on authorship ranging from Aristotle to the more recent (and dialoguing[117]) essays by Michel Foucault[118] and Roland Barthes[119], Rock questioned the need of designers to address themselves as *auteurs*, claiming they "had a bit of a dilemma overthrowing a power they may never have possessed"[120].

Unlike artists or writers, the work of designers is very rarely accomplished alone; on the contrary, artifacts of any nature are very often the result of a diverse body of skills and voices coming together to achieve the same goal. However, a number of pressures and initiatives coming from other creative fields in the last decades have brought designers to increasingly ask for a broader recognition of their work, often mistaking the notion of author with that of authority. But the idea that authorship bestows more responsibility, rights or agency is, according to Rock, a delusional fantasy rooted in the Renaissance conception of the artist as genius and which, a few centuries later,

---

[117] As one of the earliest to elaborate on the topic, Barthes' essential argument is that the author has no sovereignty over his own enunciation, which becomes devoid of any value. Barthes adopts a subversive approach to the concepts of work and authorship by envisaging the author's downfall, and advocating the role of the reader(s) to pluralise the meaning and ownership of the text. Foucault, as well, poses a challenge to the legitimacy of an unparalleled meaning in the text, but he moderates the position of Barthes by re-inviting the author to the text and conceptualizing a collective authorship.

[118] M. FOUCAULT, "What Is an Author?," in *Aesthetics, Method, and Epistemology,* ed. James D. Faubion, trans. Robert Hurley (New York: The New Press, 1999), 205–22.

[119] R. BARTHES, "The Death of the Author," in *Image Music Text*, trans. Stephen Heath (New York, NY: Fontana Press, 1977), 142–48.

[120] M. ROCK, "The Designer as Author," *Eye* 5, NO. 20 (1996).

found confirmation in the modernist interpretation of design. "If we really want to go beyond the designer-as-hero model," suggests Rock, "we may have to imagine a time when we can ask 'what difference does it make who designed it'"[121]. Clearly, the work is *always* created by someone; however, Rock's proposition is to "*embrace* the multiplicity of methods – artistic and commercial, individual and collaborative – and of people that generate the design language"[122]. According to Rock, the main challenge in the design world in the 1990s was to shift the question of "*who* made it" to that of "*what* it does and *how* it does it"[123].

After new media technologies opened up visual production and expression to an increasingly wide audience, first with phototypesetting techniques and later with the diffusion of the personal computer, design as a professional activity also faced an uncertain future. As Zuzana Licko and Rudy VanderLans wrote in the eleventh issue of *Emigre*[124] dedicated to graphic designers and the Macintosh computer, in the midst of these significant changes many designers emerged by offering new modes of development and involvement in the practice of design itself.

In particular, they highlighted how "Computer use [...] brings about a new breed of designers who possess the ability to integrate various media", while at the same time "brings up numerous previously unaddressed questions over ownership of data and our rights to use or even alter it"[125]. The title of their article, *Ambition/Fear*, captures beautifully the contrasting feeling that invested designers after the diffusion of the computer: on the one hand, a wave of excitement and creativity to aspects of

[121] ROCK, "The Designer as Author".
[122] IBID.
[123] IBID.
[124] Z. LICKO AND R. VANDERLANS, "Ambition/Fear," *Emigre*, 1989.
[125] LICKO AND VANDERLANS, "Ambition/Fear", 3.

design that have been forgotten since the days of letterpress; on the other, the uncertainty of an entire category of professionals. Two years after the release of Micheal Rock's *Designer as Author*, which originated a prolific series of debates about the future of graphic design and visual communication more in general, Ellen Lupton responded with her influential article *The Designer as Producer*[126]. In the article, Lupton feared that this renewed dispute over the notion of authorship still depended on a nostalgic idea of the writer or artist as a singular point of origin, and called for authors to become 'producers' instead of cerebral intellectuals. "The challenge for educators today", writes Lupton, "is to help designers become the masters, not the slaves, of technology" and "to seize control – intellectually and economically – of the means of production" by sharing "that control with the reading public, empowering them to become producers as well as consumers of meaning"[127].

Lupton's proactive and critical approach places itself on the threshold of the new millennium, a critical point in design history where many designers tried to re-evaluate and re-center their profession within this new and increasingly vast technological landscape. However, if one were to re-read Lupton's insight in light of the technological developments brought by new media in the last twenty years, it becomes clear that today it is almost impossible for designers to be 'in control' of anything, least of all production means. If the goal of Lupton was to turn "readers or spectators into collaborators" by revisiting Benjamin's lesson[128], today's great availability of authoring and editing tools, together with the increasing degrees of professionalization in very

---

[126] E. LUPTON, "The Designer as Producer," in *The Education of a Graphic Designer*, ed. Stephen Heller (New York: Allworth Press, 1998), 159–62.

[127] LUPTON, "The Designer as Producer", 162.

[128] W. BENJAMIN, "The Author as Producer," in *Understanding Brecht* (London: Verso, 1998), 85–103.

specific sectors of communication, seem to reverse the situation. In a visual culture where the algorithmic forces of new media exert control over communication systems and the unforeseeable digital rhizomes that are created among online users are able to generate a creative chaos of visual content, communication designers appear unable to facilitate or superintend these processes. Rather, we might be living in a new phase where designers themselves are empowered by the reading public (hence prosumers), who show designers how to integrate themselves (again) into social and political fabric.

WEATHER REPORT NR. 2

On the threshold of the new millennium, a series of great technological changes has brought to light the ever-growing role of images in Western societies, which found their legitimacy in a wide range of academic studies. Through an intensive and relentless process of mediatization, the spread of the internet has shaped the processes and discourses of political communication anew, as well as the very society in which that communication takes place. At the same time, after the introduction of new kinds of media such as laptops and editing and authoring tools, the design profession has been subjected to a series of debates about its own nature. Overall, the evolution and diffusion of new media throughout the 1990s has had an unprecedented impact on the production, distribution and reception systems of political imagery, causing great alterations both in the Western political discourse and in the role of designers willing to take part in it.

As shown in the first chapter, designers were more or less openly 'opposed' to the processes of spectacularization highlighted by Debord in 1968, and 'fought' the alienating effects of television by prioritizing the street and squares as spaces to engage citizens in political debates. However, with the increasing pervasiveness of the media in the Western political landscape, and with the influx of online users into the Spectacle's development, designers faced (and continue to face) a crisis over their modes of intervention within the political sphere. In this search for new spaces for political action, design fiction and design criticism emerged as tools of (non-)action aimed at providing the reader with a more or less speculative reading of the current social and political landscape.

At the same time, the conceptualization of an 'adversarial' design has proven critical for resurrecting a positive idea of 'conflict' in which designers do not align with political parties or institutions to 'defeat' a political enemy, but rather create spaces in which citizens themselves can mobilize and create alternatives to the current political scenarios they live in. In general, what has emerged from the design debates in the last thirty years is the will, at least by some, to re-formulate the agency of design in order to make it a practice that is not preoccupied with politics itself, but which becomes political through a radical reconfiguration of the social environment in which design practice takes place.

However, the increasing mediatization of Western politics, and in particular the use of SNS, poses a great number of challenges that go beyond the quest for a new space of action. For example, communication on SNS is meant to *appear* disintermediated, mainly through the structure of the user interface, but is in reality *ultra*-mediated through a series of mechanisms which are often ignored by online users, such as algorithms, filter bubbles, and other forms of content biases. And for a practice like design, that has long played the role of mediator between institutions or parties and citizens, the development of these processes has represented a breaking point with their past role.

As the internet became increasingly mainstream and began to show its potential for interactivity, a wide range of discourses around the role of the design field arose. In particular, several scholars attempted to reposition the attention of design not so much on the design artifact as an object, whatever this may be, but rather on the process(es) that lead to the creation of artifacts and the discourses that surround them. Thanks to this broader view, the awareness of designers has moved progressively from the spheres of production and consumption towards a more all-encompassing analysis of the artifacts' role in a given context, be they created by designers themselves or by the environment in which they operate.

Another challenge caused by the process of mediatization is the ever-increasing personalization of politics, caused by the greater legitimacy of a single political candidate within one party, the intrinsic ability of both traditional and new media to boost the visibility of party leaders, and the ever-growing capacity of online users to catalyze collective action. The dismantling of traditional political parties and the general reduction of political participation in Western countries have displaced many designers from the world of politics, who had previously viewed the collaboration with a political party as a political act rather than just a work collaboration. But also, the increasing use of SNS by political actors has resulted in the emergence of new professional figures, such as digital political strategists, who have supplanted a role previously held by designers.

And lastly, the ability of online users to create visual artifacts and at the same time mobilize a large part of the population has made digital platforms a sort of vernacular and self-contained spaces within which designers frequently struggle to integrate. On one hand, as political actors, spin-doctors, image consultants and online users all assume the role of authors in the creation of visual artifacts, design is faced with an uncertain future. But, on the other hand, this very unsettled future has made designers freer than ever to question, object to and reframe their role and purpose within the political sphere.

This change of pace was triggered by the work and writings of several design teachers and practitioners around the 1990s who, driven by the erosion of modernism's boundaries, gave rise to a slew of new questions about the relationship between author, reader, and meaning. In this context, designers have problematized the meaning of their work, offering multiple points of access to the viewer and questioning the interpretation of the artifact in relation to the authorial self. Inspired by a reconceptualization of authorship, designers began to embrace a broad range of stylistic possibilities, from informal and vernacular approaches to virtuous forms of digital image-making, which altogether guided design towards the new millennium.

From the analysis in this chapter, there are three main points which can be extracted with regard to the evolution of the Superstorm and its relationship with communication design. The first is that, in comparison to its initial stage, the Superstorm has grown exponentially in conjunction with the ever-increasing spread of new media technologies and their impact on political communication, evolving from an undefined and malleable entity into a recognized and, very often, fearsome force. Indeed, while the Superstorm was still under development between the 1960s and 1970s, the media and political landscape that has emerged since the 1990s has begun to slowly give shape to this entity – whose traces can be found in the major debates that have erupted in the same years in the fields of political theory and media studies.

The ability to account for this enigmatic force is defined by a genuine and distinct epistemological turn that has allowed images to be regarded as complex systems of interaction between visuality, appearance, institutions, bodies, and figurativeness, and, more importantly, as constitutive of a field of inquiry independent of the *Logos* – which has long prevented the image from receiving the same attention given to language. Indeed, the spread of video editing software, network technology, electronic manufacturing and many other factors has resulted in the development of new forms of visual simulation with unprecedented results, transforming the concept of a culture completely dominated by images into a technological reality on a global scale. This shift in academic attention has highlighted the fact that *what* one sees (and especially *how* one sees it) is not just a natural phenomenon, but rather the result of a series of systemic constraints which, step by step, give shape to a broader and shared field of vision.

The second is that, starting in the 1990s, this paradigm shift and the use of new analytical tools allowed the Superstorm to express itself in all its strength, allowing researchers to finally take it into account and begin to comprehend its effects. In this sense, the processes of spectacularization, disintermediation, and personalization of politics may be seen as some of the 'organs' constituting this force, demonstrating their importance in the construction of the Western political visual culture. The link between these processes is the development of political mediatization, according to which political action today takes place within the media space – or is at least heavily influenced by media activity. This new and more pronounced link between the media and political communication led to a new understanding of the power of communication strategies, resulting in significant changes in the ways political messages are produced, organized and disseminated.

The third and last consideration which can be drawn in this chapter concerns the role of communication design within the Superstorm, which began to become ubiquitous and increasingly crucial. Indeed, it is possible to observe how the Superstorm's anatomy is mostly composed of communication processes, which include image production, distribution, and consumption. On the one hand, this new focus on images, along with the introduction of new digital manufacturing systems, the internet and personal computers, has prompted the design world to reflect on fundamental issues such as agency, mediation, and authorship. On the other, however, it has been noticed how the proliferation of new tools for image creation and dissemination has increased the ability of many new actors to participate in the making of political discourse, both through hyper-professionalized communication systems as well as grass-root visual productions.

If in the early stages of the Superstorm it was still possible for designers to look at it from the outside, the spread of the internet and other new media technologies has resulted in the growth of a cyclone of unforeseeable magnitude which began to engulf society as a whole and demanded a profound re-thinking of the role of communication design from various perspectives.

III
DESIGN AND THE SUPERSTORM.
DESIGN *WITH* / *ABOUT* / *OF* POLITICS

On January 22, 2017, Kellyanne Conway, counselor to the U.S. president at that time, was invited to the weekly NBC TV show *Meet the Press* to discuss Donald Trump's recent inaugural ceremony. Over the previous days, some controversies had risen regarding the size of the crowd that had turned up to witness the event, especially after Trump himself had promised on his social media accounts an unbelievable, ground-breaking turnout. However, when it came to it, the ceremony drew a crowd only around a third of the size of that which had witnessed Barack Obama's first oath of office in 2009 (FIG. 37).

Not keen to admit defeat, the Trump administration went on the offensive and Sean Spicer, the White House Press Secretary, stated that the event had attracted the "largest audience to ever witness an inauguration, period". When Conway, on *Meet the Press*, was asked by host Chuck Todd why the secretary would utter a provable falsehood, she responded that Sean Spicer had not lied, but instead given "alternative facts". Conway's use of that phrase drew a barrage of criticism from the liberal wing of the world. Trump had of course regularly derided what he termed 'fake news' on the campaign trail, but journalists and commentators had spent the previous weeks wondering whether moving into the White House might see him begin to act in a more composed, and distinct-like manner. This episode seemed to not only disprove such theses, but also set the scene for a presidency which has often appeared to be engaged in a war with the very fabric of reality.

FIG. 37
A composite image of two aerial shots from the National Mall shows the the inauguration crowds for Barack Obama in 2009, left, and Donald Trump in 2017, right. Copyright: Emily Barnes/Getty Images; Lucas Jackson/Reuters. Source: time.com

Trump's use of visual communication in his electoral campaign and presidency, as well in many other significant political events which we will explore further in this chapter, reflects the great changes that took place in Western countries due to the increasing mediatization of the global political landscape. This period of critical transition, which took place over the course of the last two decades, has resulted in the development of a new vocabulary which describes the evolution of new and different models of representative democracy.

One of the best examples is probably the widespread use of the prefix 'post' within the ordinary political lexicon – as in the cases of 'post-democracy', introduced by sociologist and political scientist Colin Crouch in 2000 to describe a society "that continues to have and to use all the institutions of democracy, but in which they increasingly become a formal shell"[129], or in 'post-truth', defined by Oxford Dictionary in 2016 as a set of "circumstances in which objective facts are less influential in shaping public opinion than appeals to emotion and personal belief".

These changes affecting representative democracy inevitably brought about a reflection on the metamorphosis of the current political system and the crisis of mainstream parties. In fact, starting from the 1990s, many scholars have noticed how political parties and the institutions of the nation state have exhausted their potential as autonomous agents of social change, caught in the logic of informational politics and having lost much of their relevance. According to political scientist Bernard Manin, the political landscape of the twenty-first century should be understood as an "audience democracy", where the relationship between political actors and their public is established through the media and no longer through governmental institutions[130]. With this new variant of representative democracy, parties are often reduced to committees of executives who, in order to maintain their consensus, allow greater space to the personalization of politics and give life to an horizontal shaping of agreement on the use of political power through a disintermediated exchange of information with citizens.

The horizontal simplification of participation that this revolt enacts is what political scientist Nadia Urbinati defines a "live broadcasting representative democracy", which demands transparency in the way that "citizens want to see what leaders do, and they want to interact with them through the Internet and without political parties, as an audience does with the performing actors on the stage"[131].

---

[129] C. CROUCH, *Coping with Post-Democracy* (London: Fabian Society, 2000).

[130] B. MANIN, *The Principles of Representative Government,* Themes in the Social Sciences (Cambridge: Cambridge University Press, 1997).

[131] N. URBINATI, "Between Hegemony and Distrust. Representative

In the last twenty years, many political theorists have expressed concerns over the appearance of two circumstantial phenomena deriving from this new forms of representative democracy: firstly, the centralization of power in the processes of forming public opinion; and secondly, the growth of demagogic and polarized forms of consensus that split the political arena into factional and inimical groups. These, according to Urbinati, "are not extemporaneous characteristics, but rather signs of a transformation of the public sphere in mass democracies provoked by phenomena such as the erosion of legitimacy of political parties in managing representation and the escalation of economic inequality"[132].

At the same time, in the last twenty years, the forms of civic participation have been radically transformed by new media technologies, allowing citizens to become crucial actors in the forming of political discourse. Indeed, the scale of socialization inherent to politics has been immensely broadened by technological change as well as by changes at the organizational level in terms of communication strategies.

Of course, even in the "audience democracy", the party apparatus continues to have significant weight in the party itself. However, the configuration of internet structures engenders a critical reshaping of the ways in which online users operate and engage with politics and society. In this sense, social media platforms allow users to reimagine how they can participate with their *own* production on a critical level.

The increasing availability of media authoring and editing tools empowers online users to control the conceptualization of their narrative more precisely, whilst shaping a new aesthetic of visual digital content in relation to politics. This enables the establishment of new forms of relationship(s) between citizens and their political community of reference, which often leads to the

---

Democracy in the Internet Era," *Reset DOC* (blog), April 7, 2014.
[132] IBID.

creation of a deeper emotional bond between the two of them. In order to investigate these new forms of relationship established by new media, this chapter presents five case studies in which design is studied in its broadest sense and in different contexts of action, with the aim to better understand the role of design (and designers) in Western political visual culture. In this context, political visual culture is defined as the totality of the images that make up the Western political scene, together with the technologies with which those images are produced, elaborated, and distributed, the uses to which they are subjected, and the social effects they elicit.

This includes how media coverage shapes our perception of a wide range of political phenomena such as war, crises of various kinds, election campaigns, and more, or how visual performances such as military parades, national monuments, and inauguration speeches play a role in the construction of national identity. But also how movies, TV and online-streamed series, memes, social media pages, and any other visual means influence our perception of political events or political subjects through the use of explicit or non-explicit references.

As one can notice, all of these sources are very different from each other and are produced, distributed and consumed through different media. In fact, legacy media consisting of established mass media that predate the Internet – such as newspapers, radio, and television – coexist with new media that are the outgrowth of technological innovation – such as websites, blogs, video-sharing platforms, digital apps, and social media. And, as much as previous ones, the advent of these new media has brought about a transformation in language, culture, interactions among individuals, and modes of consciousness. They did so by adding to the spectrum of forms of communication – not by destroying old means of communicating[133] – and by cre-

---

[133] ONG, *Orality and Literacy*.

ating a new environment[134] where the new medium is included in the previously set ones, adding new layers of understanding to the existing set of available media together with their different institutionalizations and usages. Therefore, in order to understand how new media technologies exert influence on political visual culture through the process of mediatization, it is imperative to take them into account within the vast *media matrix* that is present nowadays.

Within this analytical framework, there are two fundamental premises that need to be considered before proceeding onto the selected case studies. The first is that the aim of this chapter is not a 'deterministic' one – in the sense that it does not focus on the 'effects' that communication design has had on the development of a particular socio-political landscape. If on one hand it is true that visual communication has increasingly become crucial in the shaping of political events, on the other it is obvious that the role played by communication design in the victory of a candidate or the success of a social movement is just an infinitesimal part of the contexts that surround events of this magnitude. For this reason, the starting point for the analysis of the case studies is not what a specific visual artifact or visual system has elicited in terms of political 'success', but rather what it can tell us about the relationship between communication design and the Superstorm. This question comprises the analysis of the circumstances under which the artifact or system was produced, the medium or combination of media utilized, and the people involved in the creation, distribution and consumption of it.

The second fundamental premise is about the use of terminology. Throughout this chapter, the word 'designer' will be used to identify anyone who adopts the means of production, consumption and distribution within the creation of the Western political visual culture. This use of the terms 'communication

---

[134] MEYROWITZ, *No Sense of Place*.

design' and 'communication designer' in their wider, most intelligible meaning is at no point meant to be provocative, but neither is it neutral. This choice represents an opportunity to scrutinize the Western political visual culture as an *ensemble* of projects within which it is possible to trace different directions, approaches and ways of using design.

In this sense, attributing the title 'designer' to artists, political strategists, and internet users is not intended to diminish the significance and autonomy of the design discipline. On the contrary, the continued and growing presence of 'people who design' in the world of politics demonstrates how fundamental communication design is today in the construction of the Western visual political culture, and why communication designers should be now more than ever involved in this dimension. The term is also employed to critically reflect on the use that designers make of design tools in relation to the uses made by other actors within the political arena. The aim here is not to make comparisons between the different uses of design, but rather look at the latter to provide an overview of how communication designers are responding to the pervasiveness of their practice and which strategies are they putting in place to actively contribute to the creation of a political visual culture of their liking.

In order to investigate the different ways in which communication design has been employed within the Superstorm during the last fifteen years, the chapter adopts three categories within which the selected case studies are located. Specifically, design *with* politics describes the collaboration between a designer or design firm and a politician or political party; design *about* politics refers to the use of conceptual and operative design tools for researching and exposing political issues; design *of* politics indicates designerly ways of conceiving, creating and managing political communication without the declared presence of any designer recognized as such.

DESIGN *WITH* POLITICS
THE 2008 OBAMA CAMPAIGN

Starting from the 1960s, the centralization of the decisions regarding media communication has increasingly become one of the main ingredients of political victory, turning the so-called 'war room' into a crucial place for political elections. Drawing on military jargon, the war room is a specific venue dedicated to the centralized management of activity planning both for the long term and at the same time used for sudden adaptations to different contingencies. Here, all professional figures ranging from pollsters to software engineers collaborate and interact seamlessly to allow the candidate to reply to the mutating circumstances of the competition in the shortest possible time. The first modern model of the war room can be dated back to Clinton's remarkable presidential campaign of 1992, which has been thoroughly documented in the eponymous documentary movie *The War Room*[135].

Directed by Chris Hegedus and D. A. Pennebaker, *The War Room* shows how the clever use of media communications allowed a relatively unknown governor from Arkansas to gain public support in a short time, overcome scandals during an electoral campaign, and eventually helped win the presidency. The lesson that can be drawn from Clinton's experience is that, when fully engaged, a successful war room becomes an adaptive organism able to change citizens' perception of the candidate, especially through choices regarding visual communication. But also, that media which rely on highly visual communication systems such as television could depict Clinton as an insurgent candidate against Bush's Republican establishment. Clearly, as Norris notes, the adoption of these practices is not

---

[135] *The War Room,* Documentary (Cyclone Films, McEttinger Films, Pennebaker Associates, 1993).

new to political communication. Indeed, after the rise of candidate-centered campaigns in the 1960s, "the move from amateur to professional campaigns was marked by more frequent use of specialist experts, PR consultants, and professional fund-raisers influencing decisions formerly made by candidates or party officials". At the same time, the rise of the modern campaign is also related to major changes in the electorate. Campaigns increasingly shifted towards "a focus that puts the 'customer' first, using research into voter's needs, wants and drives as revealed through polls, focus groups and similar techniques" to subsequently enable a "reliable service delivery on key policy issues that aim to maximize votes"[136].

The lesson from Clinton's 1992 presidential campaign was later developed further by political strategist David Plouffe, who with his team helped to lead the then-junior U.S. senator from Illinois Barack Obama into the White House. During Obama's campaign for the 2008 U.S. presidential election, there was a radical paradigm change in the foundations of political communication. At the same time, never before had design played such a critical part of a candidate's campaign.

In the book *Designing Obama*, funded with Kickstarter and published by Post Press, Design Director of the Obama campaign Scott Thomas chronicles the design process behind the work of an entire year inside the war room. Through the pages, one important factor emerges from the words of the author: that it paved the way for a new kind of interaction between design, politics and new media. Throughout the book, one can find many insights into the choices behind the development of the logo, the use of typefaces, and the overall construction of the visual identity for Obama – most of which will be etched in the history of communication design (e.g. the iconic 'O'

[136] NORRIS, "The Evolution of Election Campaigns: Eroding Political Engagement?"

logo or the use of the Gotham font) (FIG. 38). However, it is through the position the author holds in the campaign that it is actually possible to draw a line between a 20th-century political campaign and the first real transmedia campaign of the twenty-first century.

FIG. 38
Logo designed by Chicago-based Sender LLC for Obama's 2008 presidential campaign. Copyright: Sender LLC. Source: wikipedia.org

Scott Thomas, in fact, was hired with his colleague and art director John Slabyk into a working group that had never appeared into a war room before: the New Media team. The New Media team was not a part of the campaign's tech team, but rather an independent branch on par with finance, press, communication and the other ones operating in the war room. Led by political consultant Joe Rospars, the New Media team immediately became an important organ in the campaign's decision-making process, and was established from Plouffe's intuition that the internet could become the backbone of campaign functions – from fundraising to voter turnout on election day. In fact, the mid-2000s had been characterized by pivotal changes seen within the realm of communications, characterized by the introduction of social networking sites such as Youtube (2005), Twitter (2006), and Facebook (2004). By adding them to the already existing media matrix, these new platforms offered a whole new dimension to communication, while at the same time changing forever how users' information is accessed and made use of.

During their time in the war room, Thomas and Slabyk worked closely with Chris Huges, the co-founder of Facebook, for organizing and engaging with the supporters of the Obama campaign via digital platforms. Specifically there are three major changes introduced by the New Media team which, according to many, made the Obama 2008 campaign so memorable and of such great importance to forthcoming election candidates: participation, responsiveness, and candidate-centered branding. As Thomas explains in the introduction to his book, the Obama campaign recognized that "a comprehensive design strategy would be just as important as rhetoric in conveying our message", and that a critical part of their strategy would be "integrating the American people into the electoral process by forging a reciprocal and dynamic relationship with our grassroots supporters"[137]. This consideration, which might appear obvious to us nowadays, was actually another aspect of political communication that this campaign revolutionized. By introducing a successful bottom-up approach to politics through social networking sites, the New Media team was able to shape and control information about Obama's supporters in ways no other candidate had ever seen.

On the campaign's MyBarackObama.com website, for example, online users were able to create personalized accounts and produce their own web-content to be shared on other platforms, thus creating an efficient campaign-promoting strategy at (almost) no cost. User-generated content comprising videos, songs, visual art and more could be shared with one's personal network of contacts, and eventually spread virally to a broader audience. This stratagem allowed recipients of these messages to perceive this sort of communication as more reliable, creating a 'peer-to-peer' connection as opposed to the traditional vertical one.

---

[137] S. THOMAS, *Designing Obama* (Post Press, 2009), XXVIII.

At the same time, the interactive features of social networking sites, combined with web analytics, was able to provide the team with immediate feedback on the performance of their work. This is well explained in a passage of *Designing Obama*, where Thomas writes:

> "Interactive features like our campaign blog, the video diary, and individual My.BarackObama.com microsites gave us a way to make design decisions that were based on what voters really wanted, as opposed to what we thought they wanted, or what we wanted to tell them they wanted. Combined with web analytics, they gave us direct, firsthand information about what worked and what didn't, and let our design process be driven by hard data about voters' responses and opinions, not hypothetical speculations"[138].

Through this tactic, Thomas and his team were able to change any design choice regarding colors, fonts and communicative style by relying on real-time feedback provided by the citizen-users, while at the same time voicing their needs. For example, "when commenters noticed an inconsistent serif font in our 'Veterans for Obama' logo or thought that our use of a rainbow in our Pride logo looked too childish," writes the author, "I could implement changes immediately"[139].
This choice, which today could be read cynically as a system to optimize their work time regarding design choices, has been reportedly created by Thomas and his team to open the campaign to the public and to put into discussion what was being created – thus conveying the message that voters mattered.

---

[138] IBID, 50.
[139] IBID, 49.

Another last decisive aspect of the Obama 2008 campaign has been the heavier focus on the candidate's personal attributes compared to the emphasis on his policies. Portrayed through a comprehensive and coherent set of fonts, logos and colors, Obama has in fact been considered the first presidential candidate whose persona was marketed like a high-end consumer brand. On the one hand, most of the efforts were made from within the team, who not only curated all the visual material for the campaign (flyers, merchandise, information graphics, policy documents for mass distribution, posters, tickets, banners, podium signs, and placards), but also invited artists to participate in the creation of visual artifacts.

A remarkable example of this is the work by American street artist Shephard Fairey, who depicted Obama's face on stenciled red, white, and blue posters atop the word 'hope' and ended up being one of the most iconic images of this campaign and of any other U.S. campaign in history (FIG. 39). But on the other hand, to avoid the impression that Obama's image could be managed only by established artists, the New Media

FIG. 39
'Hope' poster by Shepard Fairey (2008). Copyright: Shepard Fairey. Source: wikipedia.org

team harnessed the full potential of social networking sites and opened contests periodically to allow users to produce their own merchandise and spread it with the supporters near them. For example, as Thomas writes:

> "When we decided to design a campaign T-shirt, we sent an invitation to every user who had described themselves [on the MyBarackObama.com website] using the words 'artist,' 'designer,' or 'creative'. If they wanted to submit a design, the email gave them a link that sent them to a page with the requisite visual assets so they could create a design and upload it to the site. In just a few days, we had thousands of T-shirt designs. We made the contest into a vote for 'Tees By the People, for the People,' letting users cast their ballots. The shirt with the highest number of votes won, and was available for purchase on the site"[140].

In a political scenario where candidates were represented through use of flag imagery, stars and portrait photography, Thomas' approach was able to turn for the first time in history a candidate's physical image into the object of both artistic invention and advocacy. At the same time, the launch of contests such as 'Tees By the People, for the People' on social networking sites paved the way for new and interactive modes of engaging the audience and of translating virtual initiatives into 'real' action. This was made possible by the clarity of Obama's image which, by combining a meaningful simplicity to an optimistic message, achieved a powerful synthesis of image and text and enabled civilians to share the Obama 'concept' both digitally and physically.

[140] IBID, 82.

These aspects of the 2008 Obama presidential campaign are crucial to this study because they show *how* communication design can shape political discourse and advance solutions in the management of technological resources. However, it is important to note how the solutions proposed by the New Media team for Obama's campaign, which have been praised for their innovative ability by the political world and the general public, can also be regarded as the precursors of many controversial aspects of several recent political campaigns held in Western countries.

In particular, the fact that users' participation in online politics was counterbalanced by the sharing of their own data was already showing its contradictory nature in the Obama campaign – although it actually became one of the team's leading strategies. On one hand, the pervasive use of social networking sites such as Facebook enabled a brand new way of interacting with citizens, engaging them at a deeper and more emotional level compared to traditional media. This also allowed online users to 'unleash' their potential as prosumers, who could simultaneously consume the information on the platforms and bring content and feedback to them. On the other hand, however, any supporter who logged in on Obama's campaign Facebook page or the MyBarackObama.com website could be e-mailed according to the information provided via the platform such as their age, gender, and ethnicity – thus paving the way for the process of user profiling which, as it will be shown later, will have serious implications for the future of politics.

Furthermore, as public administration expert Staci M. Zavattaro points out in her article *Brand Obama: The Implications of a Branded President*, the overreliance on branding and marketing for the construction of a political candidate could eventually give life to "hyperreal simulations" of the political experience, thus turning the candidate into "not an actual leader, but an image of leader", "not an actual statesman, but the embodied image of a national brand", "not a political campaign model, but an image-centric candidate model"[141]. And eight years later, in effect, we will be talking about the 'hyperreal' nature of future election campaigns and administrations, dusting off Baudrillard's theories on simulation[142] to provide a conceptual framework that explains a political landscape imbued with 'post-truth'.

Read today, *Designing Obama* urges us to reflect on a series of issues concerning the role of communication design and new media within the field of political communication. First of all, with all the limits that a fast-pace campaign such as this entails, Thomas has proven attentive to the role that new media technologies can play in the organization, displaying, and sharing of political information. Through a series of choices undertaken within the development of the campaign, Thomas demonstrated how design could be effectively used as a tool to implement significant changes in the shaping of a political campaign. In fact, by tapping into the zeitgeist of U.S. politics at the time, he and the New Media team were able to affect not only the way the campaign unfolded, but also the future of the Western political visual culture.

At the same time, however, many of the same techniques introduced by the team have later evolved into control and manipulation systems resulting from the increasing complexity of virtual worlds and the relentless process of mediatization brought with

---

[141] S. M. ZAVATTARO, "Brand Obama," *Administrative Theory & Praxis* 32, NO. 1 (March 1, 2010): 126.

[142] J. BAUDRILLARD, *For a Critique of the Political Economy of the Sign* (Candor: Telos Press, 1981); J. BAUDRILLARD, *The Ecstasy of Communication*, trans. Bernard Schütze and Caroline Schütze (New York: Semiotext(e), 1987); J. BAUDRILLARD, *Simulacra and Simulation* (Ann Arbor: University of Michigan Press, 1994); J. BAUDRILLARD, *The Consumer Society: Myths and Structures* (Los Angeles: SAGE, 1998).

them. When referring to the future of new media technologies within politics, Thomas was convinced that "as more and more of politics goes online, this technology can democratize the relationship between voters and politicians, making government and electoral politics far more responsive to individuals based on how they access and use information resources"[143].

Fourteen years later after this statement was made, the political situation we are experiencing unfortunately does not exactly look like this. Surely, the information resources of users are being exploited like never before by political actors – but the hope of a democratization within the relationship between voters and politicians through digital means has not yet and will probably never be reached. Thomas, on the other hand, knew something quite clearly: that when it comes to political communication and new media technologies "the medium really is the message", and that the New Media team's "use of analytics in the Obama campaign heralds a new era". "the future of politics", states Thomas plainly, "will be online"[144].

---

[143] THOMAS, *Designing Obama*, 82.
[144] IBID.

THE 2016 CLINTON LOGO

"What if... You could have it all?" So read the opening credits of the American TV series *The Apprentice*, first aired in early 2004 on the NBC network. Created by British television producer Mark Burnett, the show consisted of an unscripted drama in which sixteen American candidates from all walks of life could compete to become the head of one of Donald Trump's companies.

If anyone watches *The Apprentice* today, it is almost impossible not to link his role in the series to his success in the 2016 U.S. elections. Before *The Apprentice*, Trump had already created a considerably alluring public image as as a real estate agent in NYC (consecrated with the construction of the Trump Tower, a fifty-eight-story skyscraper in Midtown Manhattan), owner of beauty pageants (such as Miss Universe, Miss USA, and Miss Teen USA), manager of a modeling company (Trump Model Management), and face of the Trump brand selling all sorts of commercial products and services (from apparel and beverages to golf clubs). However, with an average of 20.7 million viewers each week, it is safe to assume that it was this particular show which turned him into a national popular supercelebrity.

To the cry of "You're fired!"[145], the hour-long episodes presented Donald Trump as a ruthless and infallible decision-maker who had the power to determine who would make it in the "ultimate jungle" and who would not. For fourteen seasons, aired from 2004 to 2015, Trump presented himself to the American audience as an unwavering man with business acumen willing to fulfill the ultimate (capitalistic) American dream: allowing the common man *to have it all*.

---

[145] "You're fired!" was the phrase with which Donald Trump, at the end of each episode, would eliminate one of the contestants from the race of *The Apprentice*. In American popular culture, it became the show's tagline and (one of) Trump's personal catchphrase.

In the introduction to the book *American Nightmare*, Douglas Kellner writes that the election of Donald Trump as the 45th President of the United States can be read as the culmination of the process of spectacularization – now a representative feature of the *ethos* and nature of American culture and, apparently, a factor important enough to influence election outcomes. In a context where new media (and in particular SNS) have proven to be crucial for the sharing of political views and the mobilization of the electorate, the author argues that Trump's "improbable and highly surreal candidacy" can thus be regarded as the natural continuation of his entertainment career, which moved from television screens to Twitter and eventually into the White House.

As a successful creator and manipulator of the spectacle, writes Kellner, Trump used the platform's 140-character format to "tap into, articulate, and mobilize the resentments of his followers, in a way that Democrats and other professional politicians have not been able to do"[146]. Although it may seem a bit of a stretch to compare Trump's use of Twitter to *all* other members of the Democratic Party, there are in fact plenty of studies on Trump's Twitter feed that analyze and illustrate the negative effects of his online rhetoric on the Twitter audience and its consequences on the American social and political discourse. Moreover, the persistent use of SNS in the U.S. presidential elections of 2016 also marked a new era of political campaigning, characterized by an increasingly complex, multifaceted, and networked image ecology which often sees political opponents battling with radical and polarizing views on debate topics. In this sense, the two candidates for the presidency of the U.S. government fitted perfectly into this labeling scheme,

[146] D. KELLNER, M. BRIZIARELLI, AND E. ARMANO, "Guy Debord, Donald Trump, and the Politics of the Spectacle," in *The Spectacle 2.0: Reading Debord in the Context of Digital Capitalism.* (London: University of Westminster Press, 2017), 1–13.

with Trump impersonating the populist zeitgeist and Hillary Clinton selling stability and the status quo.

Long before Trump announced his candidacy, the then-U.S. Secretary of State Hillary Clinton made a comeback in the election race. To ensure the candidate a fresh start, Clinton's 2016 campaign manager John Podesta entrusted the creation of their logo to Pentagram's partner Micheal Bierut. In collaboration with designer Jesse Reed and project manager Julia Lemle, Bierut designed a flat, blue 'H' with a red right-pointing arrow which accompanied the candidate throughout her candidacy. The idea of displaying the 'H' instead of the candidate's full name clearly draws the lessons from the logo designed by Sol Sender for Obama 2008's campaign, with a rising sun enclosed by the perfectly round 'O' set in the now-iconic Gotham typeface.

However, unlike Obama, Clinton did not have the opportunity to present herself as a brand new candidate due to her past race for the Democratic Party primary elections and her overall long-standing presence in the American political scene. In this sense, the logo had to discern Hillary Clinton not only from the other candidates in the 2016 campaign but also from her more conservative 2008 identity[147].

On April 12, 2015, when presented to the general public at the end of a two-minute video announcing Clinton's presidential run, the logo triggered a great media disdain and caused a literal 'crowdsmash'[148]. From the cartoons of the New Yorker (FIG. 40) to ironic comments on Twitter (FIG. 41) and even accusations of plagiarism by WikiLeaks (FIG. 42), people found a variety

---

[147] P. WIEGAND, "Clinton's 2016 Logo 'Fail' Not Likely to Lose Voters," Ideas & Insights | Ideas at Work, *Columbia Business School* (blog), April 14, 2015.

[148] In a *New York Magazine* article, Paul Ford (2012) coined the term 'crowdsmashed' to explain the public outrage after the release of a new logo by a company.

FIG. 40
Emily Flake, Daily Cartoon, The New Yorker. April 13, 2015.
Copyright: Emily Flake/The New Yorker.
Source: newyorker.com

FIG. 41
"Finally figured out what the Hillary logo reminds me of".
April 12, 2015.
Copyright: Nate Cohn.
Source: Twitter.

FIG. 42
"Hillary Clinton has stolen our innovative WikiLeaks twitter logo design". April 12, 2015.
Copyright: WikiLeaks.
Source: Twitter.

of similarities with other identities. Furthermore, the logo also attracted many harsh comments from design colleagues. For example, in a report by Darren Samuelsohn on POLITICO, Steven Heller claimed that "Obama's 'O' was handled with a certain amount of nuance and elegance and Hillary's 'H' has none of that nuance or elegance". In the same piece, Scott Thomas (lead designer for Obama 2008's campaign) argued that "the Hillary logo is really saying nothing. It's just a red arrow moving to the right"[149].

In his blog post *I'm With Her: What I Learned Designing a Logo for Hillary Clinton*, published in March 2017 on Design Observer, Bierut explained how the logo was intended to be "simple, open-ended, something that would invite participation", with the 'H' being "a window, capable of endless transformations"[150]. Bierut's take on the Clinton logo shows a great awareness of contemporary brand culture, where consumers notably play an active role in the creation of brand meaning. However, a 'networked' form of branding can also lead to a decentralization of brand control, where the original meaning of the logo can easily be distorted and manipulated.

As media scholar Thomas J. Billard suggests in his article *Citizen Typography and Political Brands in the 2016 US Presidential Election Campaign*, a 'simple' logo often increases the chances that consumers will creatively readapt it, while still not being altered too much from its original conception[151]. In fact, the simplicity of the logo enacted a process of transfiguration as demonstrated through the case of Hillary Bold (FIG. 43), a

---

[149] D. SAMUELSOHN, "Design Experts Trash Hillary's New Logo," *POLITICO* (blog), April 17, 2015.

[150] M. BIERUT, "I'm With Her: What I Learned Designing a Logo for Hillary Clinton," *Design Observer* (blog), March 28, 2017.

[151] T. J. BILLARD, "Citizen Typography and Political Brands in the 2016 US Presidential Election Campaign," SSRN Scholarly Paper (Rochester: Social Science Research Network, March 15, 2018).

FIG. 43
Rick Wolff, Hillary Bold. April 13, 2015. Copyright: Rick Wolff.
Source: Twitter.

FIG. 44
Patrick Mauldin, Hillary Clinton logo redesign. April 13, 2015. Copyright: Patrick Mauldin.
Source: Imgur.

typeface developed by freelance designer Rick Wolff and consisting of an arrow-adorned alphabet inspired by Bierut's logo. At the same time, it gave rise to a contest aimed at redesigning the logo through several online platforms, and saw one exceptionally popular logo suggestion going viral (FIG. 44).

In response to all this, without explicitly naming the dispute, Bierut reposted on his Twitter page an article he wrote for Design Observer in 2013 titled *Graphic Design Criticism as a Spectator Sport* (FIG. 45), where he reproached the current climate of design criticism by users as nothing less than an "endless series of drive-by shootings punctuated by the occasional lynch mob, conducted by anonymous people with the depth of barroom philosophers and the attention span of fruit flies".

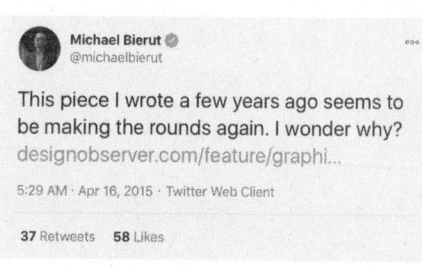

FIG. 45
Tweet by Bierut.
April 16, 2015.
Copyright:
Michael Bierut.
Source: Twitter.

It is worth noting, in the interest of full disclosure, that Trump's logo suffered a similar stroke of fate after the day of its release, on June 16, 2015. By featuring an interlocking 'T' and 'P' (standing for 'Pence', Trump's vice presidential running mate), the logo also initiated a day-long Twitter-troll fest full of several sexually suggestive GIFs and images mocking the official logo. Nevertheless, the wave of criticism about Trump's logo soon passed away, and the visual representation of his campaign was cleverly replaced a few months later by the emphasis on the slogan 'Make America Great Again!'. Besides, the slogan found its way of dissemination through a truly curious artifact: the MAGA hat (FIG. 46).

First worn by Trump at the World Trade International Bridge in Laredo (Texas) on July 23, 2015, the bright red hat emblazoned with the words 'Make America Great Again' has now become part of the Western cultural landscape. As anthropologist Barbara Jones brilliantly points out, "Instead of becoming a 2016 campaign relic, disappearing onto the shelves of junk shops and other purveyors of Americana, [the MAGA hat] became an expression of ideology that now tends to either offend or hearten those who see it"[152]. In contrast to this analysis, which recognized the hat as an object of study both from a socio-political and anthropological point of view, Michael Bierut dismissed it as "nothing more than a red hat with a badly kerned, caps-locked slogan"[153].

FIG. 46
Baseball cap associated with the 2016 presidential campaign of Donald Trump, with the text 'Make America Great Again'.
Source: wikipedia.org

In itself, the Clinton logo has nothing 'wrong' with it. What is questionable, however, is how the designers who managed the overall campaign communication positioned themselves within the socio-cultural context that surrounded the 2016 elections. As is well known, Trump's candidacy announcement during the early summer of 2016 appeared as surprising as much as unlikely to most of his (soon-to-be) political opponents. And yet, since the outcome of the Brexit referendum vote, one could easily sense that the 'unfeasibility' of certain political scenarios deemed 'improbable' by surveys and polls needed to start being taken seriously.

---

[152] B. JONES, "The MAGA Hat, a Curious Artifact of Contemporary America," Anthropology News 60, NO. 4 (July 2019).
[153] BIERUT, "I'm With Her."

If one is to understand the logic of Trump's 2016 campaign, it is necessary to place it within the context of a mediatized politics that merges political discourse and entertainment – of which Trump is a perfect example – and which cannot be ignored. As a media persona, Trump combines all of the features of the Spectacle and often treated political issues as if he was playing a role in *The Apprentice,* mixing politics with a form of entertainment typical of reality television which American viewers were fairly familiar with. Trump's rhetoric then becomes obvious in the show-like dimension of his rallies and writings, which emphasize performance over factuality. Indeed, as political scientist Kenneth Cosgrove observes in his article *The Emotional Brand Wins*, during his campaign "Trump offered highly visual solutions to the nation's problems: building a wall, tearing up free trade agreements, banning Muslims from entering the country and using signs of his wealth and business experience to show that he alone could clean up Wall Street and turn the country around"[154].

Moreover, Clinton's communication strategy was heavily outmaneuvered by Trump's collaboration with British political consulting firm Cambridge Analytica, which built an entire technological infrastructure to create predictive models of the audience that Trump needed to engage with. Through a series of weekly polls, the data collected provided the means to track the electorate, and was able to show which countries had the highest number of persuadable voters, which social and political issues appealed to which members of the target audience, and segment them according to how they were likely to behave. By profiling users' personality characteristics based on their social media profiles, Cambridge Analytica was able to deliver

---

[154] K. COSGROVE, "The Emotional Brand Wins," ed. Anastasia Veneti et al. (Poole: The Centre for the Study of Journalism, Culture and Community, 2016), 27.

1.4 billion impressions[155] in just four months (July - November 2016) across four thousands separate ad campaigns, and contacted about 150,000 people, sending them highly targeted digital video content[156]. According to Cambridge Analytica's CEO himself, targeted communications were able to deliver 11% increase in favorability and 8% in voter intent for Trump[157].

What is interesting to note is how Bierut, in light of these events, has polarized the debate as a mere win-lose situation by often looking at his job as if that logo was just another brand to be designed among the list of the illustrious others he represented. Stating that Donald Trump's graphics "combined the design sensibility of the Home Shopping Network with the tone of a Nigerian scam email" and complaining that "it isn't pleasant to have talk-show hosts making fun of your work on national television"[158], raises questions on what it actually means for designers to be involved in political discourse.

This also applies to Clinton's campaign communication director Jennifer Kinon (co-founder of the branding and design agency OCD), who led a team of sixteen designers over a sixteen month period after Bierut, Reed and Lemle completed their task. When Suzanne LaBarre, editor of Co.Design, interviewed her in the aftermath of the election's outcome asking, "Do you feel like you approach your practical work differently from more traditional client work?", Kinon replied, "No, because our client work is based almost entirely on our understanding of the audience and user, and we approach political work the exact

---

[155] An impression is a metric used in online marketing strategies to quantify the number of digital views or engagements of a piece of content. Also known as 'view-throughs', impressions usually refer to the times that users see a targeted advertisement any time they open an app or website.

[156] A. NIX, "From Mad Men to Math Men" (YouTube Video, Online Marketing Rockstars Keynote | OMR17, Hamburg, March 10, 2017).

[157] NIX, "From Mad Men to Math Men."

[158] BIERUT, "I'm With Her."

same way [...] By nature we are agnostic – we'll work in any industry"[159].

Meanwhile, in March 2017, just two months after Donald Trump's controversial inaugural speech, the CEO of Cambridge Analytica Alexander Nix was invited at the Online Marketing Rockstars Festival in Hamburg to deliver a speech on the role played by his consulting firm in Tump's 2016 electoral campaign. During the presentation, titled *From Mad Men to Math Men*, Nix illustrated the techniques used to gather data for the campaign and how psychographic segmentation has helped he and his team to target voters based on shared psychological characteristics[160].

Apart from the issues concerning the precarious ethics of CA's methods – for which Nix was to face the court in the following year – the keynote actually highlights a point that is highly relevant to understanding how communication design is seen outside its bubble. At 5:40 minutes, Nix states that:

> "Big data is fundamentally changing the way that communications are undertaken. Back in the 1950s, the era of *Mad Men*[161], creativity was top-down – that is brilliant minds came up with

[159] J. KINON AND B. MARTIN, *Design Has A Huge Role To Play In Politics, Even If It Can't Win An Election*, interview by Suzanne LaBarre, Video, April 28, 2017.

[160] According to the Swiss newspaper *Das Magazin*, the methods of data analysis of CA are to a large extent based on the academic work of Michal Kosinski, who in 2008 joined the Psychometrics Centre of Cambridge and developed with his coworkers a profiling system able to analyze the behavior of users through their 'likes' on Facebook and other social networking sites. The system, called O.C.E.A.N, divides users according to the features of openness, conscientiousness, extraversion, agreeableness and neuroticism. Reference article: «Ich habe nur gezeigt, dass es die Bombe gibt». Source: tagesanzeiger.ch

[161] Mad Men is an American TV series aired from 2007 to 2015.

> creative concepts and they pushed them onto an audience in the hope that they would resonate. But today, we can use big data to understand exactly what messages each specific group within a target audience needs to hear way before the creative process is even started"[162].

This part of the speech is really intriguing because it alludes to the demise of 'creatives' in political communication management in favor of companies like his that deal with big data. Also, it is interesting to note how the example set by Nix skips from the 1950s to 2017, as if the world of design within the field of political communication has not evolved since.
Clearly, Nix's point of view is highly biased due to his involvement within Trump's 2016 electoral campaign. However, it is reasonable to question whether designers working in the political realm are still convinced that *any work* can be framed in a commercial sense. And even if the world of design research has been pointing for decades to new forms of design whose purpose is precisely to deal with contemporary social and political dynamics – whether to describe, overturn, or problematize the current state of things – the attention paid to the Clinton logo by the design editorial world and the considerations of designers in relation to election results expressed in interviews seem to show the opposite.
The fact that Nix uses the famous television series *Mad Men* as a metaphor for understanding the evolution of the world of communication is no coincidence, of course. On the contrary, one of the reasons the show has achieved such popularity over time is probably because it offers us nostalgia as a lure, capturing and monumentalizing on the screen a gilded age for communication design. This crucial aspect of the series is not concealed by the director; on the contrary, it is expressed through the word of

---

[162] NIX, "From Mad Men to Math Men."

the protagonist, Don Draper, who in the context of a business meeting during the thirteenth episode of the first season says:

> "Nostalgia – it's delicate, but potent.[...] It's a twinge in your heart far more powerful than memory alone. This device isn't a spaceship, it's a time machine. It goes backwards, and forwards... it takes us to a place where we ache to go again. It's not called the wheel, it's called the carousel. It lets us travel the way a child travels – around and around, and back home again, to a place where we know we are loved"[163].

This famous quote from the show can be considered as a sort of meta-reflection that Don is posing both to himself, to the business partners sitting at the table with him, and to the viewers of the show. On one hand, Don is a character that is unable to fully assimilate into the rapidly changing present, chased by restless memories of the war and family matters. However, *Mad Men* also articulates the viewer's potential nostalgia for being part of an era of hope and radical change such as the 1960s in the U.S. When applied to the world of design, it is easy to see how the shimmering world portrayed in *Mad Men* (or, more accurately, the show's interpretation of the changes occurring in the advertising industry during the 1960s – now known as the 'Creative Revolution') may represent for designers a safe haven in today's chaotic and complex world. The idea that a single man has the power to deliver outstanding pitches that could later become the next popular brand's tagline brings us back to a lost capitalist paradise in which the work of a creative 'genius' could make an impact on a global scale. However, the 1960s have proven to be the prelude to a series of radical changes that

---

[163] From *Mad Men*, season 1, episode 13.

would have creatives falling off the building of capitalist wealth – just like the retro title sequences of *Mad Men* – into an abyss of dubious and desperate memories.

Today, faced with a series of incomprehensible social and political disasters, it may seem convenient to take refuge in comforting scenarios where the dynamics of the world appear clearer and uncompromised. However, it might be precisely the confusion of our times that could drive the scope of design, shifting designer's attention from the glossy appearances of political imagery to the invisible tensions that generate it – along with all the difficulties this entails.

DESIGN *ABOUT* POLITICS
STEVE BANNON: A PROPAGANDA RETROSPECTIVE

In 2018, the British former political operative Benjamin Harnwell started renovating a 13th-century monastery known as Certosa di Trisulti in a secluded and rural setting in Collepardo, Frosinone province. However, the monastery was not intended to be a luxury residence for the English lobbyist. The aim was to turn the entire charterhouse into what Harnwell defined a 'gladiator school'. The school, named 'The Academy for the Judeo Christian West', was expected to take in fifty to three-hundred European students a year and teach them how to defend Christianity, Western values, and the art of far-right politics. In the same year, Belgian lawyer and far-right politician Mischael Modrikamen founded a think-tank called 'The Movement'.

The masterplan behind The Movement was to bring structure to the various populist movements and parties in Europe. The organization planned to link up with thirteen emerging or established far-right parties to help them win seats in the European Parliament and legitimize their Eurosceptic vision in the old continent. These experiences have been both attributed (both financially and in terms of ideas) to Steve Bannon, the man behind Trump's successful communication strategy during the U.S. elections of 2016. In fact, after he was fired by Trump[164] and even shunned by his far-right website Breitbart News[165], Bannon decided to take his talents across the Atlantic, where he tried to lead a far-right renaissance. Bannon's interest

---

[164] Bannon was asked to leave the White House in August 2017 after months of reported power struggles with Trump's son-in-law and senior adviser, Jared Kushner, as well as other high-level Trump advisors. Trump had also reportedly grown weary of press leaks and of Bannon taking credit for his election victory.

[165] Bannon stepped down from his position at Breitbart News in January 2018, where he had served as Executive Chairman since 2012.

in these organizations stems from his recognition of the populist wave that was gaining momentum in several Western countries at the time, such as the withdrawal of the United Kingdom from the European Union, the formation of the yellow-green government[166] in Italy, and the growth in popularity of far-right movements all across Europe.

What is interesting about Bannon's figure is that he has never been formally recognized as a campaign strategist. However, as a right-wing new-media entrepreneur, he has been able to build a political and news infrastructure that attracted both Trump as well as many European nationalists leaders. Bannon's image has often been associated with that of an 'aggregator' by journalists and media outlets, but often too little attention was paid to his ability to create (and sell) an imaginary, thus leaving unanswered the question of who Steve Bannon really is. To this query, Dutch artist Jonas Staal has answered unequivocally: he is a 'propaganda artist'.

In his doctoral thesis, titled *Propaganda Art from the 20th to the 21st Century*[167], Jonas Staal addresses the topic of propaganda by questioning its relationship with art practices. Contrary to common belief, Staal believes that the meaning of the term 'propaganda' should not be confined to the power structures of the 20th century, but rather be expanded to the modern and contemporary political scene. By defining propaganda as "a performance of power with the aim to construct reality for its interests", Staal also shuns any derogatory connotation to the term. In this sense, the artist claims that our global political reality includes a plurality of competing propagandas, and that propaganda as an art form could and should be utilized as a transformative practice capable of changing the (political) order of things.

---

[166] The name derives from the colors associated with the parties of the coalition, M5S and the Lega.

[167] J. STAAL, "Propaganda Art from the 20th to the 21st Century" (Doctoral Thesis, Leiden University, 2018).

Throughout the thesis Staal recognizes mainly three kinds of propaganda, identified within the categories of 'War on Terror Propaganda Art', 'Popular Propaganda Art', and 'Stateless Propaganda Art', and which altogether construct our global and manifold political reality. Written in a period of escalating political tension all over the Western world, Staal's thesis offers not only a compelling interpretation of the role of propaganda in the 21th century, but also and above all a key to reading the political dynamics that followed the UK's departure from the EU in the summer of 2016.

Shortly after publishing his doctoral dissertation, Staal teamed up with the Director of Research and curator Marina Otero Verzier of Het Nieuwe Instituut (Rotterdam) for the exhibition *Steve Bannon: A Propaganda Retrospective*, held from April 20 to September 23, 2018. Stemming from Staal's research on propaganda, the exhibition aimed to show the prolific production of images designed by Steve Bannon, who went from being a Goldman Sachs venture to the head of Trump's campaign in the U.S. presidential elections of 2016. In the exhibition, Staal presents the work of Bannon within the framework of "contemporary propaganda art developed through the public–private infrastructures of the expanded state[168] that produces images of imminent societal destruction and survival through the Us/Them dichotomy"[169].

Through a careful cataloging and analysis of Bannon's production, Staal introduces him to the public as a unique and genuine artist. To achieve that, the exhibition is structured in five phases, each showing a specific period of Bannon's formation

---

[168] "With regard to the expanded state", says Staal, "we speak here of the government-driven military-industrial complex and the private economies it includes, which have shaped the massive infrastructures of the War on Terror". Staal, "Propaganda Art from the 20th to the 21st Century", 206.

[169] IBID, 290.

as an image-maker: I. From Hollywood to September 11, II. Bannon' Cyclical Time, III. From Tea Party to Alt-Right, IV. Cultural Marxism, and V. Performing Trumpism (FIG. 47–50). Through the dissection of Bannon's works, Staal encourages a retrospective glance at how the Us/Them divide structures itself through visual representation.

FIG. 47–50
Installation views of *Steve Bannon: A Propaganda Retrospective* by Jonas Staal and curated by Marina Otero Verzier. Copyright: Jonas Staal, Marina Otero Verzier, Het Nieuwe Instituut (Rotterdam). Photo Credits: Nieuwe Beeldenmakers.

In this respect, Staal emphasizes how 2004 represented a pivotal year in Bannon's experience as a visual storyteller with the production of the biopic *In The Face Of Evil: Reagan's War In Word And Deed*. Based on Peter Schweizer's book *Reagan's War* (2002), the movie follows a thread from World War I to the fall of the Twin Towers, focusing especially on totalitarian regimes and their aftermaths. According to the script, all of these atrocious experiences connect back to 'The Beast', an embodiment of "Nietzsche's will to power" that feeds off "man's dark side" to achieve the "control of the state and power as an end unto itself". Throughout the movie, Reagan is portrayed as a dedicated hero against the Soviet Union, and thus as the combatant of one of The Beast's many faces. But at the same time, the historical excursions taken throughout the movie lead the viewer to experience the evolution of The Beast, which shifted from being embodied in Communism to the fringes of 'Islamic terrorism'. "Bannon's message is clear", says Staal in relation to the final meaning of the movie: "a new Reagan is needed to wage an unapologetic war in the face of this cyclical return of evil"[170].

The last chapter of the exhibition explores Bannon's influence on the rhetoric of the Trump's administration as Chief Advisor of the White House, as well as his forced departure from it. One of the most interesting features of Staal's work within this exhibition is the depiction of the imagery produced by Bannon as seemingly disparate and yet highly consequential. In fact, each phase of Bannon's image-production is framed as cyclical, which is able not only to yield insightful interpretations of the different kinds of zeitgeist behind the scenes, but also to anticipate the evolution of contemporary Western political rhetoric.

Towards the end of the exhibition Staal displayed *The Disappearance of Steve Bannon*, a work consisting of two juxtaposed photographs (FIG. 51). The first one portrays Trump and Bannon with a park ranger in Pennsylvania, the second one Trump alone with the park ranger. Through this set of photographs, Staal recounts the fleeting, derelict, and ambiguous nature of Bannon, who remains ethereal and elusive just as the imaginaries that he creates. At the same time, Staal indicates that the creative propulsion at the heart of Bannon's work is self-destructive, causing him to frequently seek out new challenges and new shores.

---

[170] J. STAAL AND M. O. VERZIER, *Steve Bannon: A Propaganda Retrospective By Jonas Staal* (Rotterdam: Het Nieuwe Instituut, 2018), 20.

FIG. 51
Jonas Staal, *The Disappearance of Steve Bannon* (2018). Produced by Het Nieuwe Instituut (Rotterdam). Copyright: Jonas Staal.

If the work of Staal is 'unorthodox' in many ways, so is the operation of Otero Verzier. In fact, by exhibiting the work of Steve Bannon at Het Nieuwe Instituut, the curator shows how the fields of design, architecture, and digital culture are as vital for the formation and dissemination of political ideas as they are for their disruption. To begin with, Otero Verzier clearly states how designers and related cultural environments "have the responsibility to operate beyond politically-minded bubbles"[171]. To achieve this purpose, Het Nieuwe Instituut hosted a series of lectures, presentations, and debates before and after the inauguration of the exhibition aimed at discussing the implications of propaganda with a variety of hosts. This approach established the basis for the establishment of an agonistic arena where conflict could peacefully happen and differences be confronted.
Secondly, the exhibition addressed contemporary challenges such as the spread of the alt-right and its cultural practices at a time when the populist discourse was more active than ever, both in the Netherlands and in many other European countries. The decision to operate in the 'here-and-now' is not coincidental, but rather reflects the Institute and the curator's desire to open a space for dialogue and confrontation on such timely issues.

[171] IBID, 6.

"Shaped by the volume and speed at which information circulates and by which dominant narratives are constructed", says Otero Verzier in fact, "this deceiving territory demands a visual literacy: a competence in reading images, spaces, and objects"[172].
Lastly, the idea of concentrating the focus of the exhibition on Bannon's work challenges the canonical definition of authorship, questioning who is an artist in this context and who is not. By presenting the exhibition as a 'retrospective', Otero Verzier invites reflection on this word, which might have not been used solely in artistic terms (as in a compilation of an artist's works overtime) but also as an effort to retroactively trace the roots of Trumpism (and populism more in general) as a visual phenomenon.

One of the most interesting aspects of this exhibition is that, through a series of ingenious display choices, the curator and the artist bring to life a sort of 'construction site' where the populist rhetoric is built. The populist language, known for its strong and dismissive tone, has always been (and continues to be) the subject of many studies in academia. However, in addition to analyses related to the study of its formal structure and use by political actors, a great number of scholars have ventured into the study of the meaning and broader goals of the use of this rhetoric. This is the case, for example, for academic and populist expert Paul Taggart, who in the early 2000s conceptualized what he defined 'the Heartland' to better reflect what populists often mean in their rhetoric[173].

According to the author, the Heartland is a *locus amoenus*, an ideal place "in which, in the populist imagination, a virtuous and unified population resides"[174]. The populist 'Us' is born precisely here, from this chimeric 'reign' which represents a

---

[172] IBID, 8.

[173] P. TAGGART, *Populism* (Maidenhead: Open University Press, 2000).

[174] IBID, 95.

shelter against globalization, a remedy for the complex modern world, an idealization of society. It is here that the citizen, alone, imagines what is still to be created and thus foreshadows a political experience. According to Taggart, the imagined reality of Heartland "celebrates a hypothetical, uncomplicated and non-political territory of the imagination"[175].

In this sense, the concept of the Heartland emphasizes that the people in the populist rhetoric are neither real nor completely fictional, but rather figure as a sort of mythical subset of the whole population. From this fictional and imaginative place, individuals draw their values, establishing a vision of what society should look like but also one of those who do not contribute to its actualization. In fact, if the Heartland is necessary for individuals to build a vision of what the 'Us' or 'the People' look like, it also adds a further element crucial to the nature of populism, that is the identification of the 'Enemies of the People', or 'Them'. As the populist mental universe is structured in a dichotomous and manichaean form, the 'Enemies of the People' represent those who do not correspond to the ideal image of what populists think their members should look like, and who grow apart from the core values upon which populism is based.

If the Heartland formulated by Taggart constitutes a theoretical speculation on the nature of the populist rhetoric, which has been revised and updated by many academics in the coming years, Staal and Otero Verzier's work represents a valid visualization of it. With the exhibition *Steve Bannon: A Propaganda Retrospective*, Staal and Otero Verzier reminded viewers that the power of visual narratives is not limited to seeing or recalling scenarios appearing in one's personal experience. On the

---

[175] P. TAGGART, "Populism Has the Potential to Damage European Democracy, but Demonising Populist Parties Is Self-Defeating," *EUROPP, The London School of Economics and Political Science* (blog), December 13, 2012.

contrary, they skillfully display how the populist rhetoric (and propaganda more in general) uses imagination as a medium to stage politically significant meanings related to either memories of the past, diagnosis of the present, or imagined futures. Any movie, picture, YouTube video or meme can reflect the viewer's innermost thoughts and become a building block for a shared yet unspoken collective scenario, which can become a powerful asset in the hands of politicians.

Deconstructing propagandistic and populist narratives should not be intended as the act of imposing one's ideas on someone else, but rather as providing the tools for the viewer to comprehend (and maybe oppose) the construction of an ideology. If Western societies actually find themselves "in the midst of a culture war"[176], then Otero Verzier and Staal show the design and art fields which weapons to take up – and the viewers how to join the battlefield.

---

[176] STAAL AND OTERO VERZIER, *Steve Bannon: A Propaganda Retrospective By Jonas Staal*, 6.

DESIGN *OF* POLITICS
THE BEAST

Whilst modern campaigning has been characterized by the professionalization paradigm[177], post-modern campaigning sees a hyper-professionalization that leads to actual trends or styles of conducting a campaign. In a way, it could be said that the increasingly escalating levels of technological sophistication shifted post-modern campaigning from the "wisdom of the war room"[178] to the wisdom of the political strategist. As seen in the previous case study, names like Steve Bannon are acquiring an increasingly important role in the way political actors are depicted through visual means, and they seem to attract a greater amount of media coverage over time. However, if Bannon served Donald Trump for only seven months and managed to make the headlines quite a few times, there are other political strategists who operate in the dark, helping politicians to run their communication on a daily basis and contributing to shaping the overall communication lines of EU's populist parties.

In Botteghe Oscure's street, at number 54 and right in front of the building that was once home to the Italian Communist Party, resides today the right-wing party Lega and its communication staff – *la Bestia* ('the Beast') (FIG. 23). *La Bestia* refers to the social networking machine that operates 24 hours a day, 7 days a week behind the online communication of 'the

---

[177] J. G. BLUMLER, D. KAVANAGH, AND T. J. NOSSITER, "Modern Communications versus Traditional Politics in Britain: Unstable Marriage of Convenience," in *Politics, Media, and Modern Democracy: An International Study of Innovations in Electoral Campaigning and Their Consequences*, ed. Paolo Mancini and David L. Swanson, Praeger Series in Political Communication (Westport, Conn: Praeger, 1996), 49–72.

[178] M. SCAMMELL, "The Wisdom of the War Room: US Campaigning and Americanization," *Media, Culture & Society* 20, NO. 2 (April 1998): 251–75.

Captain', aka Lega's leader Matteo Salvini. Ideated and managed by entrepreneur and self-proclaimed 'digital philosopher' Luca Morisi, *la Bestia* sees the collaboration of more than thirty digital experts who cover Salvini's public and private life with the constraint of absolute confidentiality about their identity and their work. Since 2014, *la Bestia* has been at the heart of Salvini's communication strategy, and has helped him increase both his visibility and number of electoral votes – to the point of obtaining the position of Interior Minister after the elections of March 2018.

One of the most visible contributions that *la Bestia* has brought to the communication of Lega has probably been the massive rebranding of the party's image, which has been critical to the party's resurgence. In fact, the party has risen from 4% of votes cast in the 2013 Italian general election to 34% in the 2019 European Parliament election. At the heart of this victory is a significant shift in the party's position, which went from being a local party with a relatively small audience (then called Lega Nord, 'Northern League') to one of the most acclaimed sovranist and anti-European parties on the Western political scene.

One of the most clear references for the Lega's rebranding has been the French populist colleague Marine Le Pen, who has been able to transform the niche movement created by her father (called Front National) into a nationally recognized political party – now Rassemblement National. During French political elections, posters hanging all over the streets of France featured the campaign slogan *Au nom du peuple* ('In the name of the people') and the words *MARINE Présidente*, accompanied by a blue, thorn-free rose. What was gone was Front National's red-white-and-blue flame logo and most importantly the image of Le Pen's father, Jean-Marie, who had no place in this metamorphosed, new and re-branded party. According to Jérôme Fourquet, director of the French opinion polling firm Ifop, by presenting the candidate by her first name, Marine

Le Pen and her communication team "tried to create a closeness and suggest a product that is less hard, less worrying, less frightening"[179].

Similarly, the Lega Nord ('Northern League') has been gradually losing its status as the 'Party of the North,' and began to define a less regional and territorial positioning in favor of a more national and international one. Following Marine Le Pen's example, Lega completed a set of moves that led to a rebrand aimed at gaining a more voter-friendly and all-encompassing image. First of all, the previous nominative Nord ('Northern'), which was preceding the word Lega, was removed. Like Marine's purpose of erasing the well-consolidated image of her father, so Salvini was trying to delete Italian's memories of Umberto Bossi, former leader of the Lega Nord (1991-2012) and promoter of the idea of transforming Italy into a federal state, with fiscal federalism and greater regional autonomy – especially for Northern regions like Lombardy, Veneto and Piedmont.

The whole concept of this rebranding campaign revolved around the extreme personalisation of the party through the figure of its leader. This is extremely visible in the management of the logo, which included the modification of the old one as well as the addition of a new one. Most notably, Lega's logo went from having the word 'Padania'[180] at the bottom of the circle to have the words 'Salvini Premier' instead – thus moving the centrality of the party from its geographical roots to its leader (FIG. 52, 53). At the same time, a brand new logo was created to be used in most of the social media pages of Salvini,

---

[179] Fourquet in Kim Willsher, "The Family Name and Party Logo Have Gone but Can Marine Le Pen Detoxify Her Brand?," *The Observer*, January 7, 2017, sec. World news.

[180] Padania is an alternative name and a proposed independent state encompassing Northern Italy, derived from the name of the Po River, whose basin includes much of the region, centered on the Po Valley, the major plain of Northern Italy.

displaying only the words 'Salvini Premier' and therefore excluding entirely the name of the party from the composition. Not surprisingly, this logo draws heavily on the one adopted from Trump's 2016 electoral campaign, both in the use of color, typography and positioning of the tagline (FIG. 54, 55).

FIG. 52
Lega Nord's logo from 1991 to 2017.
Copyright: Lega Nord. Source:
wikipedia.org

FIG. 53
Lega's logo for the 2018 general election.
Copyright: Lega Salvini Premier. Source:
wikipedia.org

FIG. 54
Trump's 2016 election campaign
logo. Copyright: Donald Trump for
President. Source: wikipedia.org

FIG. 55
Lega's logo for the 2018 general
election. Copyright: Lega Salvini
Premier. Source: wikipedia.org

Apart from the rebrand of the party's image, *la Bestia* is well known for taking advantage of new media technologies to create ad-hoc images that are posted on all of Salvini's social media channels multiple times per day and that changes according to the specific case and the contingent situations. The way *la Bestia* works is fairly simple, yet very effective.

Firstly, the production of images is heavily based on polls, which are continuously conducted by Italian analyst firm SWG. Images are created based on a monitoring system that tracks the sentiment of Italians and identifies the most discussed topic of the day, therefore allowing the leader to adapt the content and tone of messages accordingly. For example, in an investigation conducted by the Italian TV show *Report*, journalist Giorgio Mottola found out that the Lega commissioned SWG to test voters' perception of white supremacist skinheads[181]. As polls showed that 67% of Salvini's electorate did not consider them to be particularly dangerous[182], the Lega leader was then able to be photographed in public with the leader and team of *CasaPound* – an Italian neo-fascist movement.

Secondly, members of *la Bestia* follow the leader everywhere – whether physically or virtually – and this gives life to a sort of delocalized war room which produces a great amount of live content. During campaign rallies, for example, the members of *la Bestia* are divided equally between stage and backstage: some are filming the leader for a Facebook Live event, some are taking photos, and others are quickly editing the pictures into the designated formats to share them with the social media channels of the Captain (FIG. 56).

---

[181] From the investigation by Giorgio Mottola conducted for the TV show *Report* titled *La fabbrica della paura* (in english 'The factory of fear'), aired in October 2019. Source: rai.it

[182] From the study *Osservatorio permanente sull'opinione pubblica 2017–2018 | SPECIALE NAZISKIN* conducted by the Italian market research and consulting firm SWG.

In the same way, when participating in a TV show, Salvini often addresses the camera well aware that *la Bestia* is meanwhile grabbing live content for other channels (FIG. 57).

FIG. 56
Pictures by Luca Morisi showing how la Bestia operates during a campaign rally in Maranello.
January 18, 2020.
Copyright: Luca Morisi.
Source: Facebook.

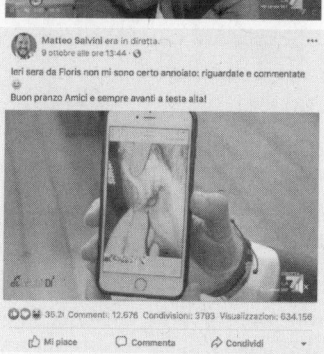

FIG. 57
Matteo Salvini shows to the cameras of TV show DiMartedì the picture of a prison guard's ear that was allegedly bitten by an immigrant prisoner, later reposted on his Facebook page.
October 8-9, 2019.
Copyright: Matteo Salvini, DiMartedì (LA7).
Source: Facebook, LA7.

Thirdly, *la Bestia* relies heavily on the use of posting patterns and visual templates, which have been often labeled as 'ridiculous' but that nonetheless have become one of the most recognized features of Matteo Salvini's style of communication. Specifically, there is growing evidence that in situations of difficulty for Salvini (or one of the Lega's other members) a certain type of imagery goes online. When scandals come to light, when the Captain is not performing well (especially as he held the office of prime minister), or simply as a boost before election day, Salvini's Facebook page immediately fills up with images of cats, food, and pictures with his youngest daughter (FIG. 58, 59, 60). This move has proven to be an effective deterrent to move the attention of Salvini's electorate away from news reported on traditional media, but has also elicited criticisms from the opposition parties who have often accused him of superficiality in addressing the real problems of the country.

FIG. 58 – 60
Examples of pictures posted on Matteo Salvini's Facebook page containing cats, food and pictures with his daughter. Copyright: Matteo Salvini. Source: Facebook.

And lastly, the visual communication created by *la Bestia* is systematically organized through the use of graphic templates, which have now become a common and widespread component of any Italian political leader. In particular, Lega's leader mainly uses two Facebook pages to carry out a double strategy. On his personal page, he posts edited pictures that quote journalists who express themselves in his favor, shows headlines of right-wing online newspapers, and uses montages that defame members of the ruling government (FIG. 61). Conversely, on another page named *Matteo Salvini Leader*, mainly followed by fierce voters for the party, the collaborators of *la Bestia* inform users about the appearances of Lega's members on TV shows to boost their records (FIG. 62).

FIG. 61
Examples of pictures posted on the Facebook page Matteo Salvini Leader informing users about the daily appearances of Lega's members on Italian TV shows. Jan 26 – 24, 2021. Copyright: Matteo Salvini.
Source: Facebook.

FIG. 62
Examples of pictures posted on the Facebook page showing journalists who express themselves in his favor, headlines of online right-wing newspapers, and montages that defame members of the ruling government. Dec 30 – 29, 2020. Copyright: Matteo Salvini. Source: Facebook.

If these four aspects represent (or at least are part of) the strategic creation and organization of Lega's long-term visual content, *la Bestia* also sporadically engages in the creation of short-term experimental campaigns in crucial moments of Italian politics. One memorable campaign in this regard is the *Vinci Salvini* contest ('Win Salvini'), which was launched on the leader's Facebook page on February 6, 2018, almost a month before Italy's general elections scheduled on March 4[183].

Vinci Salvini was an online game based on a very simple principle: the quicker one 'liked' Salvini's new Facebook posts, the higher were the chances to engage with the leader. Based on the speed with which they put 'like' on a post, users were awarded points. The game awarded 500 points for the first 10 likes, 250 points for those up to 100, 200 points for the first 1000, and so on. The 'daily winner' won a post with their picture posted on all of Lega's social networks and a phone call with Salvini. The winners of the four weekly rankings won a meeting with Matteo Salvini himself and a video of that event was published on the Facebook, Instagram, Twitter, and YouTube pages of the leader (FIG. 63).

To participate in the game, users needed to create a profile on the website vincisalvini.it by going through two steps: first, logging in using a Facebook account, and then filling out a form with personal information. In addition to social media accounts, the users were also asked to provide a valid email address and a phone number. This mechanism exploited the rules of dissemination of the posts used by the algorithms of Facebook, allowing the dissemination of Lega's political communication online. At the same time, the personal information provided through the website allowed *la Bestia* to profile registered users and to target them with specific communications according to their age, gender, and place of origin.

---

[183] A second edition of the game was launched on May 9, 2019, just a few weeks before the 2019 European Parliamentary election – held between 23 and 26 May, 2019.

FIG. 63
Example of two young winners of the contest *Vinci Salvini* showing support for Lega's leader. In return for their loyalty and participation in the campaign, they got their picture posted on Salvini's social media accounts. Copyright: Matteo Salvini. Source: Facebook.

By merging political engagement and gamification, *Vinci Salvini* marked a step ahead in the direction of personalization and spectacularization of the Italian political leadership[184], demonstrating once again the endless possibilities of political engagement inherent in new media technologies. *Vinci Salvini* is a perfect example of how the user can be turned from the spectator into the actor of political communication, from the object of political attention to the subject of it. At the same time, the political actor is deprived of any political meaning and turned into what the Spectacle demands him to be: a product to be advertised (FIG. 64).

[184] In the U.S., gamification had already been used as a tactic to disseminate political messages and gather data at the same time. For example, when senator Ted Cruz ran for the Republican Party's presidential nomination in 2016, he launched the Cruz Crew app, through which supporters could win prizes by inviting friends, donating funds, and sharing the candidate's thoughts through a series of game levels which went from 'Intern' to 'Revolutionary'.

FIG. 64
Promotional video for the second edition of Vinci Salvini. May 9, 2019.
Copyright: Matteo Salvini.
Source: Facebook.

The settlement of Lega and *la Bestia* (today no longer under Morisi's leadership)[185] in Via delle Botteghe Oscure, which has been a symbol of the Italian Communist Party for many years[186], was not intended as a symbolic gesture. Nonetheless, it carries a powerful poetic meaning. In the so-called 'First Republic' – a national journalistic term referring to the Italian political period that goes from 1948 to 1994 – the party headquarters played a crucial role, and no party would have accepted having its own next to that of a rival. In the context of Western contemporary politics, the Lega's gesture is not provocative, but rather symptomatic of a system that is shifting its space of action in the most literal sense. The transition of democracy from an 'explicit' to an 'implicit' space is one of the most distinguishing features of the Information Age, which by nesting politics among its circuits gives birth to systems through which our political life takes shape that are intangible, invisible – in fact, we could say – obscure.

[185] In September 2021, Luca Morisi left his position as manager of *la Bestia* after being investigated by the Prosecutor's Office of the city of Verona for trafficking and possession of drugs during a night spent in his apartment with two male escorts met through a dating app.
[186] Via delle Botteghe Oscure literally translates to 'Obscure Workshops Street'. The street owes its name to the several economic and artistic activities that were windowless, and therefore obscure. Since the Italian Communist Party had its headquarters in this street for more than fifty years, it was called for years by party members and the press as *Bottegone*, that is 'Great Workshop'.

LE BIMBE DI GIUSEPPE CONTE

On March 11, 2020, the World Health Organization's director-general, Dr. Tedros Adhanom Ghebreyesus, declared the novel Coronavirus outbreak a global pandemic. On the same day, Italy's Prime Minister Giuseppe Conte tightened lockdown measures over the entire country, shutting down all commercial and retail businesses except for pharmacies and food retailers in the effort to halt the coronavirus outbreak. Since then, it has become clear that the state of emergency caused by COVID-19 did not only raise concerns over economic and health-related problems in Italy, but also that the quarantine and the anxiety-inducing flow of information through the media proved to be a trigger for a series of concerns ready to undermine the population's sense of security, and temporarily compromised the freedom of individuals to determine their future.

To cope with this situation, Italian political actors and institutions tried to make sense of an unexpected (and yet unresolvable) situation through a plethora of narrative expedients, primarily of a visual nature. The prevailing narrative has been the one adopted by the Italian government and scientific institutions, who identified the virus as an 'enemy'. This discourse was built around a series of visual expedients which accompanied Italians throughout the quarantine months, and eventually made them hopeful and willing to follow rules established for security and health purposes.

The most glaring example of this narrative strategy were probably the daily press conferences by the Italian Civil Protection, where department head Angelo Borrelli informed the Italian population on the course of the pandemic through the number of people infected, those in intensive care, and the deaths caused by the virus. This series of meetings was live-streamed in Italy for fifty-five consecutive evenings beginning February 23, and eventually created a sort of collective ritual where Italians could hear the opinions of prominent experts on the evolution of the pandemic.

Another kind of narrative is the one fielded by Italian political actors, both internal and external to the government who, perhaps due to the impossibility to carve out a space in any news media, resorted to SNS to make their voices heard in the midst of the media discourse. In a context dominated by fear and the absence of clear information, alarmism quickly turned into a mechanism of spectacularization, often expressed through the instrumentalization of news for political gain and through the adoption of 'argutainment'[187] as the preferred style of debate in media representations. Political actors adopting this communicative strategy mostly staged narratives that could generate feelings of belonging and exclusion by either defending the demands of citizens or by standing against governmental decrees and scientific positions on the management of the crisis during the months of the Italian lockdown (March-April 2020).

Among these it is possible to find the governor of the Veneto region and Lega member Luca Zaia commenting on the supposedly "unspeakable" Chinese health and hygiene standards

---

[187] According to political communication theorists Paul Saurette and Shane Gunster (2011), 'argutainment' is one of the debate styles most used by populists to spread their political agenda, and is considered by the two as "a provocative and entertaining style of debate, defined as highly emotional and passionate, strongly opinionated, simple and brief and very confrontational" (P. SAURETTE AND S. GUNSTER, "Ears Wide Shut: Epistemological Populism, Argutainment and Canadian Conservative Talk Radio," *Canadian Journal of Political Science / Revue Canadienne de Science Politique* 44, NO. 1 (2011): 195–218, 205). Argutainment is based on a communicative strategy that aims at producing bellicose statements, and it is used by political actors both to attract visibility and consensus as well as to contest knowledge authorities. For these reasons, the authors argue that argutainment often achieves a strong response in media debates.

on venetian TV channel *Antenna* 3, the video accompanied by the #milanononsiferma (*#milanwontstop*) hashtag posted by democratic Milanese mayor Giuseppe Sala who refused to close commercial and retail businesses in his city, the constant mood swings of Matteo Salvini (leader of Lega) with respect to the management of the pandemic crisis (inciting first the closure of borders, then their immediate reopening), the attacks of Luigi Di Maio (leader of Movimento 5 Stelle, 'Five Star Movement') on French satirical videos mocking Italy as the first european country affected by the pandemic (followed by an adjoining institutional meeting with the french ambassador in Italy to express formal apologies), the conspiracy theories expressed by Giorgia Meloni (leader of Fratelli d'Italia, 'Brothers of Italy') regarding an alleged plan against Italy to undermine the export of italian products, and many more.

During the months of the quarantine, however, it was not only politicians who shaped the debate around the crisis generated by the pandemic. Italian online users also fabricated spontaneous forms of communication to ease and give meaning to their experience of the pandemic, while simultaneously enabling a networked identity-building process. Instead of framing an 'enemy' as many political actors did, online users designed a conspicuous number of memes around the figure of Italian prime minister Giuseppe Conte on social media, creating a sort of collective support system to face the mandatory quarantine period. Starting in March 2020, prime minister Conte entered the media scene by establishing a ritualized cycle of meetings streamed on his Facebook page and which, although delivered in audiovisual format and despite all the historical and social differences, somewhat resemble the fireside chats held by Roosevelt on the radio in one of the darkest periods in American history.

The first of these was released on March 4, where Conte explained the reasons behind containment measures, calling for the respect of safety procedures, and asking citizens to address a time of unprecedented crisis with resolution. Lasting for five minutes and shot at around eight pm in Conte's office at Palazzo Chigi, the live video had a good response in terms of views and user engagement. However, it was a second video that, perhaps for the measure of its message, triggered something in the Italian online audience towards their PM that was to last for the whole quarantine period.

On the evening of March 11, after Conte's live stream on Facebook in which he announced the tightening of lockdown measures across the entire country, a conspicuous number of memes, gifs, and social media pages flourished online, all dedicated to Italy's PM (FIG. 65). Among these, the case study will mainly analyze the Facebook page *Le bimbe di Giuseppe Conte*, which by re-framing the political figure of Italy's Prime Minister as a hot, funny, and reassuring man gave life to a curious phenomenon of 'political fandom'.

The concept of political fandom has been studied more intensively over the last decades by many academics from a wide range of fields, mainly focusing on the significant overlap between fan communities and the increasingly mediatized world of politics. The roots of this phenomenon are inextricably tied to the personalization of politics, partially caused by the ever-increasing presence of political actors on media channels[188]. And, although the personalization of politics and the phenomenon of fandom have always existed, even on so-called traditional media (such as television and radio), the diffusion of SNS in the last two decades has extended the area of political action to new players as well as to new forms of expression.

Overall, like pop-culture communities, political fan communities have proved to be effective in the "emotional constitution

---

[188] E. ERIKSON, "'Hillary Is My Friend': MySpace and Political Fandom," *Rocky Mountain Communication Review* 5, NO. 1 (2008): 3–16.

FIG. 65
Search results for 'Giuseppe Conte' on Facebook (2020). Source: Facebook.

of electorates that involves the development and maintenance of affective bonds between voters, candidates, and parties"[189]. When fandom applies to politics, one is usually confronted with the (co-)creation and consumption of new aesthetic forms capable of broadening the means of political engagement and developing a sense of collective or subcultural identity around shared tastes – usually achieved through a bottom-up process promoted by prosumers[190].

---

[189] L. VAN ZOONEN, *Entertaining the Citizen: When Politics and Popular Culture Converge* (Rowman & Littlefield, 2005), 66.

[190] M. M. BROUGH AND S. SHRESTHOVA, "Fandom Meets Activism: Rethinking Civic and Political Participation," *Transformative Works and Cultures* 10 (June 15, 2012); C. SANDVOSS, *Fans: The Mirror of Consumption* (Malden: Polity Press, 2005).

Political fandoms, in this sense, have the power to establish "imagined communities"[191] fostered by technologies that "enable geographically dispersed people to overcome time and distance in forging virtual communities of affect"[192]. SNS are crucial in this process not only because they allow people from diverse locations and cultures to come together and form a community, but also because they can create bonds of collaboration.

By leveraging the power of "collective intelligence"[193], political fandoms on SNS lead to collectivistic participation in political activities through effective mobilization of skills. In this regard, online fan-like forms of engagement with politics affect not only the ways political images are produced and shared but also the relationships between the agents involved in these processes[194]. Indeed, social media are able to establish "affinity spaces", defined by the American linguist Gee[195] as informal and highly generative environments, from which new aesthetic experiments and innovations emerge. Eventually, these forms of engagement have the power to influence not only the way in which political visual content is produced and shared, but also the relationships between the agents involved in these processes. The page *Le bimbe di Giuseppe Conte* was created by a girl named Marta, who thanks to the collaboration of many online

---

[191] B. ANDERSON, *Imagined Communities: Reflections on the Origin and Spread of Nationalism* (London: Verso Books, 1983).

[192] L. HITCHCOCK MORIMOTO AND B. CHIN, "Reimagining the Imagined Community: Online Media Fandoms in the Age of Global Convergence," in *Fandom: Identities and Communities in a Mediated World*, ed. Jonathan Gray, Cornel Sandvoss, and C. Lee Harrington (New York: NYU Press, 2017), 174.

[193] P. LEVY, *Collective Intelligence: Mankind's Emerging World in Cyberspace* (New York: Perseus Books, 1997).

[194] H. JENKINS, *Convergence Culture: Where Old and New Media Collide* (New York: NYU Press, 2006).

[195] J. P. GEE, *Situated Language and Learning: A Critique of Traditional Schooling* (New York: Routledge, 2004).

users was able to create a parallel and imaginary world devoted to the figure of Italian PM through the tool of meme. Indeed, even though it was Marta who effectively supervised the creation of contents and selected the memes posted on the page, the production of the posts was entrusted to the page's followers for the entire period of the quarantine.

The page was created on March 12, 2020, and saw one hundred seventy memes published between March 12 and April 24, 2020, with an average of 3.8 memes posted per day. The first part of the page's name, 'Le bimbe di' ('*The baby girls of*'), mocks a fandom model typically dedicated to Italian influencers or famous people, which involves the creation of a social network page containing either unposted content related to these public figures and/or memes commenting their latest activities. Of the one hundred seventy memes posted on *Le bimbe di Giuseppe Conte*, one hundred and thirty-one are made by Facebook users, who are credited either in the post description or in the first comment as 'bimba' or 'bimbo' (in English: 'baby girl' or 'baby boy') (FIG. 66, 67).

FIG. 66, 67
The creator of *LbdGC* credits users for their content: a mask with Conte's face and a picture of him with the inscription "Peppe take me and put me in quarantine" (2020). Copyright: LbdGC. Source: Facebook.

The memes posted in *Le bimbe di Giuseppe Conte* follow for the most part a camp aesthetic, and as such show a strong sensibility for "artifice and exaggeration"[196]. In particular, the memes produced by both the creator of the page and Facebook users adopt the trend of "self-aware kitsch", which sees "the makers themselves [...] aware of their 'bad taste'", and works therefore as a parodic stand to mass culture[197]. Judging by the formal features of the memes (which include many heart emojis, scribbles, stickers, and Conte's face applied to other pictures), it can be assumed that they were created to a large extent with photo-editing apps for smartphones and with Photoshop or other desktop applications. The memes of *LbdGC* are characterized mainly by the presence of low quality, highly modified images which could be categorized in three categories: photomontages of Giuseppe Conte in various situations, drawings sent by fans, and pictures of self-produced merchandising (FIG. 68, 69, 70).

FIG. 68 – 70
Example of photomontage, drawing and picture of self-produced merchandising (2020). Copyright: LbdGC. Source: Facebook.

[196] S. SONTAG, "Notes on Camp," *Partisan Review* 31, NO. 4 (1964): 515-30.
[197] M. MEYER, *The Politics and Poetics of Camp* (London: Psychology Press, 1994), 182–183.

The messages of *LbdGC*'s memes are commonly a mixture between wordly tributes to Conte's physical features, his choices on the pandemic crisis, and his imaginary platonic love for the 'bimbe' – a combination as unexpected as effective. In general, the in-joke within the followers of the page is based on the idea that Giuseppe Conte is actually aware of the existence of the 'bimbe', and that he secretly considers himself as their 'sugar daddy'. The intention to create an alter ego of Conte's figure is encapsulated in the nickname 'Peppy', which is used sarcastically by the 'bimbe' in reference to a tweet that Donald Trump published on 27 August 2020, where he had initially misspelled Conte's first name as 'Giuseppi' (from there → 'Beppi' → 'Peppy').

Taken together, the one hundred seventy posts of *LbdGC* during the quarantine months achieved 239,283 reactions, 34,158 comments and 34,621 shares, with an average of 1407.5 likes, 201 comments and 204 shares per day. Clearly, we may assume that is the combination of the memes' subject, together with the use of vernacular elements by fans, and the exceptional historical period that allowed the sprouting of this and many more fandom phenomena around the figure of Giuseppe Conte. In fact, after the live-streamed speech on Facebook by Conte on March 11, a conspicuous number of fan pages emerged on other social networks, together with fanfictions on Wattpad, lo-fi playlists on Youtube, and even PornHub categories (FIG. 71, 72, 73). In this sense, it is interesting to note how *LbdGC* did not represent an isolated experience, but rather the culmination of a series of fan-based artifacts produced during the months of quarantine toward the Italian prime minister.

The case study of *Le Bimbe di Conte* fits into a particular context where, as mentioned in the introduction, Italian citizens dealt with a period of exceptional emotional difficulty dictated by the state of the quarantine. The fact that the fan page was born the day after Conte's announcement of a national lockdown

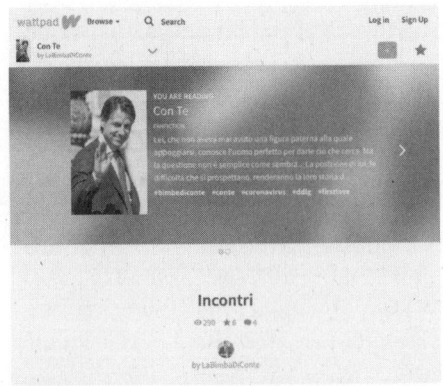

FIG. 71
Fanfiction based on Giuseppe Conte's life (2020). Copyright: LaBimbaDiConte. Source: Wattpad.

FIG. 72
Playlist lo-fi on Youtube inspired by Conte (2020). Copyright: Shunsuke Nakamura. Source: YouTube.

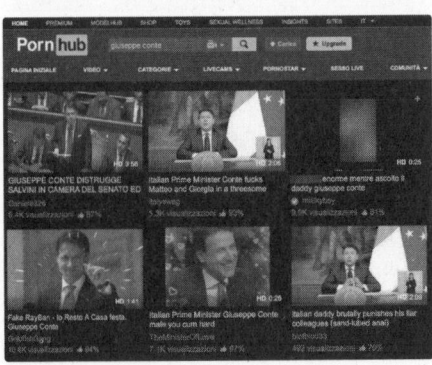

FIG. 73
Search results for 'Giuseppe Conte' on PornHub (2020). Source: PornHub.

leads us to believe that the processes that lead to the creation of political fandom might be extremely visceral. In fact, if on one hand the explicit aim of the page is to create a form of visual entertainment, on the other hand there must also have been – both by the creator of the page and the audience – an awareness of the role of images and their capacity to generate a sense of community. In addition, *LbdGC* has been a triumph of prosumers and their ability to establish a coherent visual language without the guidance of any 'creative director'.

Lastly, the memes created in the page gave life to a real reframing of the political figure of Conte, who went quickly from having a controversial role in the Italian political scene to being the object of flattery (albeit in a humorous form). By picturing Italy's PM as a hot, funny, and reassuring man, online users thus (re)organized the audience's experience into interpretative frames[198] and influenced the transfer of information from the producer to the consciousness of the receiver[199].

This phenomenon, although clearly very minimal within the political debate that took place during the months of the quarantine, is reflected in the growth figures regarding the growth in popularity of Conte. In fact, according to a survey conducted by market research and consulting firm Ipsos for the Italian newspaper *Corriere della Sera*, between April 22 and 23, 2020 the approval ratings for the Italian government marked an increase of five points for PM Giuseppe Conte (from 61% in March to 66% in April) and two points for the Government (from 56% in March to 58% in April).

---

[198] E. GOFFMAN, *Frame Analysis: An Essay on the Organization of Experience* (Boston: Northeastern University Press, 1986).

[199] D. A. CROW AND A. LAWLOR, "Media in the Policy Process: Using Framing and Narratives to Understand Policy Influences," *Review of Policy Research* 33, NO. 5 (2016): 472–91; R. M. ENTMAN, "Framing Bias: Media in the Distribution of Power," *Journal of Communication* 57, NO. 1 (2007): 163–73.

Since the onset of the government, these indexes mark the highest approval ratings ever achieved by the government and the PM (in January 2020 approval ratings for the government was 45% and 50% for the PM). Regarding the leaders of main Italian parties, the survey marks a major shift: leaders of opposition parties recorded a decrease of approval ratings, whilst political figures within the country's governing coalition showed an increase of ratings, with Giorgia Meloni (leader of Fratelli d'Italia, 'Brothers of Italy') decreasing by four points and Matteo Salvini (leader of Lega, 'League') down by three points[200].

Today, the Facebook page of *Le bimbe di Giuseppe Conte* no longer exists (†, date unknown), leaving room for many new fan pages still active under different creators' management – such as the eponymous @lebimbedigiuseppeconte on Instagram, which today counts more than 270,000 followers. Taken together, *LcdGC* and the other fandomic episodes which emerged during the months of the quarantine reveal how online users are taking on greater importance in the representation of contemporary politics. And, while still in an embryonic stage, political fandoms seem to be slowly opening the way to new dialogic forms of participation where grassroots communities have the possibility to give life to new group forms thanks to new media's affordances. Clearly, given the transience of such phenomena, it is currently almost impossible to understand to what extent virtual communities fulfill a role in the political scene and/or if they are able to influence the electoral behavior of citizens.

---

[200] Specifically, compared to the previous month Matteo Salvini – leader of the Lega lost 5,7%; Giorgia Meloni – leader of Fratelli d'Italia lost 6%; and Berlusconi – leader of Forza Italia lost 1%. On the contrary, Luigi di Maio – politician of Movimento 5 Stelle gained 2%; Roberto Speranza – politician of Articolo Uno gained 4%; Franceschini – politician of Democratic Party gained 2%; and Teresa Bellanova – politician of Italy Italia Viva gained 2%.

In this specific case study, for example, it is much more safe to assume that it has been the increase in Conte's approval ratings that gave life to the fandom phenomenon, and not vice versa. Almost as if the race at infotainment online during the quarantine, characterized by the necessity to make viral daily current affairs, took an unexpected and definitely more creative turn than usual. And this because, in the end, fandoms fully represent the sort of phenomena which mysteriously appear on the internet: funny catalytic forces, which we often overlook, but that step by step give silently form to the dynamics of our everyday digital life.

WEATHER REPORT NR. 3

The analyses in the five case studies in this chapter help us outline an entirely new scenario of Western politics, dictated by an ever-evolving (and unpredictable) visual landscape. What seems evident is that, over the past fifteen years, design has always been present in the processes of political communication – albeit through very different forms. However, in the nets of the Information Age, a greater number of human and algorithmic actors are giving life to a multifaceted production of visual artifacts in a jumble of professionalism and bottom-up activity in which designers seem to have little to no space for action.

In the section on design *with* politics, I have investigated the status of 'traditional' commissioned work in the realm of politics and its implications in design discourse. The first case study, focusing on the work of Scott Thomas within the New Media team for Barack Obama's 2008 presidential campaign, shows how Thomas and his team were able to introduce a series of innovative techniques which can still be found in today's management of political communication. At the same time, it is also possible to observe how the enthusiasm that characterized the creation of these new systems of engagement – driven by the hope that new media technologies would be able to democratize the relationship between voters and politicians – has unfortunately faded over time, turning these same systems into controlling and manipulative weapons in the hands of contemporary politicians.

The second case study under this category examined the contribution of Michael Bierut to Hillary Clinton's 2016 electoral campaign, focusing in particular on the various discourses that surrounded the logo during the election period. On one hand, this showed how the launch of the logo elicited a multitude of different reactions by the online public – thus proving, whether mocked or praised, that the candidate's logo was not overlooked by voters. However, on the other hand, it showed how some of the most popular designs for online media centered the whole election debate *just* on the logo itself, either by blaming or commending Bierut's work, almost making it seem like the logo alone could really have an influence on the election results. In the same way, Bierut has repeatedly written online articles about the alleged 'superiority' of his logo compared to Trump's campaign imagery, relying only on what was visible of the two opponents' campaigns. In a political landscape marked by the use of advanced microtargeting techniques and other data-mining system implemented in the creation of Trump's campaign, it seems as if the competition with the rival's imagery has caused Bierut's project to avoid dialogue with the complexities of the new media system, shutting itself in a sort of design autarchy which eventually materialized into a project whose narration resulted culturally decontextualized.

For the purpose of this study, it is not relevant to look at the Clinton logo as the 'smoking gun' behind the 2016 elections outcome. On the contrary, the case study wishes to demonstrate how the insistence on the authorial debate about the artifact (brought forth by some of the world's most influential online design magazines and the designer himself) prevents it from broadening the perspective on the role that design has played in these elections. The fact that online users felt so deeply involved in the choice of Clinton's logo, in fact, demonstrates how the visual aspects of political communication are still important for voters. On the other hand, it is clear that the creation of images in the ultra-mediated and highly responsive context in which Western politics finds itself demands a space for debate that can go beyond the questions of 'who created it' and 'has it worked or not', possibly broadening the scope and critical assets of the practice of design.

Het Nieuwe Instituut's exhibition *Steve Bannon: A Propaganda Retrospective* by artist Jonas Staal and curated by Martina Otero

Verzier falls into the category of design *about* politics and reads, of course, as a completely different experience from the ones listed above. One of the most interesting aspects of this work is probably the reverse perspective on the issue of authorship, which is reflected in the term 'retrospective' in the title of the exhibition. In fact, by displaying and re-organizing Steve Bannon's visual production, Staal steps aside from the position of producer and assumes that of the 'archivist', helping the viewer to reflect on the kind of imagery that dominates our contemporary political sphere. At the same time, by bringing this exhibition in a museum dedicated to the fields of design, architecture, and digital culture, Otero Verzier invites a reflection on how these disciplines are of vital importance for the dissemination and disruption of political imaginaries. Furthermore, the fact that the exhibition was open just one year after Trump's election and at a time when the populist discourse was extremely active in Europe shows the curator's vision and intention to use the museum as an open space for dialogue and confrontation, a public agora where contemporary political challenges can be addressed. As it is often the case with exhibitions, it could legitimately be said that, by looking at political communication only as a research object and within the walls of a museum, projects such as this one might forsake the opportunity to co-shape the direction of political change. However, even if these long-standing considerations are currently still valid and need to be taken into account, one has to wonder *how* designers can do such a thing and most importantly *if* this possibility still exists nowadays.

The third category, design *of* politics, comprises two case studies that are both frighteningly close and somewhat ironically distant from those analyzed so far. Through a massive rebranding of the party, the use of templates and unusual gamification techniques, *la Bestia* can help us understand what the most extreme extent of candidate-branding and microtargeting could eventually lead to: an invisible system of forces driven by entertainment and rewards. Unlike any of the previously examined case studies, Morisi's project operates in the long-termn, and thus is able to constantly adapt its strategies to the new kinds of media emerging within the media matrix. When compared to the other case studies, *la Bestia* leads us to wonder if this new system of self-perpetuating 'semipermanent' political campaigning will increase even further and, if so, how designers can actually intervene in it.

Le Bimbe di Giuseppe Conte, on the other hand, can be considered a glorious triumph of prosumers. Compared to the work of Thomas, Bierut, and Morisi, this experience has highlighted the ability of users to establish a coherent visual language without the guidance of any 'creative director', supervisor, or form of control. The messages of *LbdGC*'s memes are commonly a mixture between wordly tributes to Conte's physical features, his policy choices on the pandemic crisis, and his imaginary platonic love for the *bimbe* – which works at the same time as a strong bonding agent and a parodic stand to mass culture.

Even if the explicit aim of the page was to create a form of visual entertainment, the memes created in the page gave life to an actual reframing of the political figure of Prime Minister Giuseppe Conte, who went quickly from having a controversial role in the Italian political scene to being the object of a (although humorous) form of flattery. By picturing Italy's PM as a hot, funny, and reassuring man, online users (re)organized the audience's experience into interpretative frames, thus becoming a spontaneous and virtual reflection of changing citizen preferences. This case study, which has radically different characteristics from the ones analyzed above, was included in the research mainly as a provocation. It is unclear to what extent the content of this page can actually be considered important in the scenario of Italian politics during the pandemic, and yet what is clear is that these phenomena – as random as they may be

– are starting to happen unexpectedly and increasingly often. The aim here is not to award these situations merits that they do not really bear, such as 'diverting' voters' choice. However, acknowledging their existence and trying to understand their potential and impact, as well as their possible consequences for the world of communication design, might be useful in light of the ongoing expansion of the activity of online users with the field of political communication.

Through the analyses in these five case studies, it is possible to see how over a span of eight years the landscape of political communication has changed dramatically, together with its interaction with the field of design. If in Thomas's work for the 2008 Obama campaign we could catch a glimpse of possible new alliances between design and politics through new media, the case study of *Le Bimbe di Giuseppe Conte* leaves us with a world where it seems impossible to understand the mechanisms governing the production of visual artifacts related to politics, let alone control their future development. In this chapter the Superstorm is operating at peak capacity, embracing political communication and new media technologies in its vortex to the point where they become a single driving force which increases the complexity of the Western political visual culture. At this point of our journey, the only thing left to ask is how, and if, design will be able to confront it in the future.

CONCLUSIONS

At this point of our journey, after we have seen the Superstorm grow exponentially over the last sixty years, it is natural to wonder *how* and *if* it is possible to weather it. In particular, it is reasonable to wonder whether, based on the historical, critical, and cultural analyses conducted in the three chapters, it is possible to trace the guiding lines for a sort of 'navigation manual'. Although the idea of providing a guidebook is very appealing, I believe that any systematic or otherwise solution-oriented approach would be inadequate in the face of the problems presented in this book – especially given the complexity of the relationship between political communication and new media technologies.

I am making this point specifically as I believe that this inadequacy is symptomatic of a conception of design that is now far removed from the reality designers actually live in, but which nonetheless still appears to predominate within design discourse, reflecting itself in the bold titles embroidered with shiny typefaces that promise 'solutions' to the issues of our zeitgeist. However, the single assumption that complex issues such as capitalism, the Anthropocene, the patriarchy, the climate crisis or, as in this case, the Superstorm, may be overcome, confronted, or 'resolved' through a manualistic approach (often expressed in the proposition 'how-to-something') is only one of many consequences of a cultural system which, probably, should be focused on posing the right questions instead of giving answers.

It is worth noting, for example, that terms such as 'capitalism' or 'Anthropocene' are already postulatory exercises in and of themselves and, since they are sensitive to the zeitgeist that permeates them, possess an intrinsic semantic and ontological slipperiness. It follows that confronting words that are actually systems in constant flux through a recapitulatory and purposeful approach rarely helps to understand the complex nature of a term – and neither the variety of meanings that this may acquire depending on the context in which it is used. In this book, for example, the word 'Superstorm' already represents the attempt to describe a complex system of forces through a narrative metaphor and that, due to its evolutionary nature, is and will always be in a constant state of change.

For the reasons listed above, the conclusion of this book will not provide an operating manual for navigating the Superstorm, and neither will it state what designers can and cannot do in order to overcome it – assuming that this is even possible. Entering this territory would be, if I may be excused a pun, like indicating to wear a life vest in case of a plane crash: an act that makes us hope for survival but does not guarantee it, at all.

Unfortunately, when confronted with the Superstorm, there are no life vests, oxygen masks, escape hatches nor shelters. There is, however, the possibility of understanding its logics in order to formulate a new understanding of the position that designers can assume towards it and, eventually, face its relentless effects.

OLD WEAPONS, NEW STRUGGLES

Throughout the chapters of this book, we have seen how the Superstorm is an ephemeral entity which develops in time and space, able to increase exponentially in size as the years pass by. In the Superstorm, the role of time and continuity are crucial, since the parts that constitute it may be considered as an updated version of what came before. In this sense, the 'challenges' that the Superstorm poses to Western democratic systems are always new and evolving, but also contextually historicizable. However, as evidenced by the case studies, it seems quite clear that designers are often employing 'old' tools to address extremely current issues. This concept, which also gives the title to this paragraph, is an excerpt from an editorial piece written by designer and researcher Francisco Laranjo in the third issue of Modes of Criticism, titled *Design and Democracy*[201]. The passage from which the phrase is taken is more extensive, and reads as follows:

> "While we curate Instagram moments, stories and cute boomerang loops, xenophobic and fascist messages pour from Twitter to the streets and Ivanka is branded as universal female role model. The #Brexit General Elections are celebrated with leopard loafers and yearning for another season of Downton Abbey with a Nigel Farage cameo. Everything is information and counterinformation – purposefully staged contradiction.
> Yet, we designers, made some powerful pins to put on our jackets to reach our own cheerleading team. We made fun of Trump's hair, hands, mouth, plane, tower and gold before he was even elected, without tickling the system. *We're using old weapons for new struggles*, often overlooking the importance of collective action. We made DIY banners look stronger, more urgent and effective than anything we do or have traditionally done. We made satiric design powerless and subvertising pointless"[202].

[201] F. LARANJO, ED., *Modes of Criticism: Design and Democracy* (Eindhoven: ONOMATOPEE, 2017).
[202] IBID, 4–5.

This short extract highlights a key point of this book, which I attempted to address especially in the third chapter through the case studies presented, and which concerns the designer's position towards the Superstorm. The lesson one can draw from this chapter is that turning our backs on the Superstorm in search of an ideal political world is no longer an option today. It was in the 1960s, when designers tried using the space of the streets to activate processes of collaboration and mobilization around a shared issue, and it might have been in the 1990s, when an uncertain future allowed the design field to experiment with new ways in the field of political participation, but it is certainly not the case today. Avoiding the Superstorm today means to wilfully disregard an entire system of political meaning production that, although once impalpable, today violently manifests itself on a daily basis through its effects.

Certainly, the interaction with the Superstorm does not have to be 'direct' at all costs. There are, as we saw with the case of *Steve Bannon: A Propaganda Retrospective* in the category design *about* politics, a number of systems that allow the use of design tools to expose the Superstorm, make it visible, analyze it, and, as a result, confront it. But the museum is not and should not be the only place where this may happen. The use of digital tools, employed not only for the production but also for the dissemination of political messages, is an example of an area that is yet relatively unexplored but with enormous potential. However, as the case of *Le Bimbe di Giuseppe Conte* showed us, entering into these bottom-up production processes that belong to the category of design *of* politics often means overlooking many of the logics that are currently used within the design field, ranging from production systems to artifact distribution to the non-exclusive conception of authorship, as well as the issue of financial needs. In the same way, I believe the category of design *with* politics presents a valid series of opportunities for designers today, as long as they are addressed while paying scrupulous attention to the Superstorm. Indeed, the case of Obama's 2008 presidential campaign demonstrates that it is possible to conceive of a design approach that is well aware of the potentialities and limits of new media technologies through a proactive and critical stance.

However, as it happened in this very case, it is clear that adhering to this category entails the acceptance of a wide range of risks, including the inability to predict the effects of certain choices in the future, as well as a high level of media attention focused on one's own work. In any case, as I emphasized in the third chapter, what matters is not which category designers work in but rather, as Laranjo points out, which 'weapons' they bring into play.

FOR A POST-NOSTALGIC PRACTICE

To understand the reasons behind the stalemate between communication design and political communication, it is necessary to return to the analysis of nostalgia within the field of design, which I briefly mentioned in the third chapter, and to the three issues of agency, mediation and authorship analyzed in the second chapter. In fact, although many designers have already addressed these issues, particularly from the 1990s onward, it appears that a rethinking of these issues is now required – at least within the context of the Superstorm.

The issue of agency is perhaps the most contentious, as it requires a reflection on the role that designers might play in shaping the Western political debate. As shown through the analyses of Obama and Clinton's electoral campaigns, it is quite common in the mainstream design discourse to link the work of designers to the victories or defeats of political candidates. However, this aspect linked to performativity often steers the field of design in a deterministic and anti-analytical direction.

In fact, even if it has been proven that visual communication plays an essential role in the field of politics, it is crucial to remember that this is only one small part of the myriad of factors at play in political outcomes. Therefore, rather than focusing on the effects that communication systems might elicit within a socio-political context, what is more interesting is the analysis that precedes and follows the design act in a given context. In this sense, the book *Designing Obama* can be considered as the result of an important collection of thoughts and reflections but which – almost certainly – would not have seen the light if the candidate had not been elected to the presidency of the United States. To the same extent, it is legitimate to speculate that if Hillary Clinton had won the elections, we would now have a hardcover volume containing pages and pages of praises for the communication systems that would have granted her victory and the long-awaited entry into the White House.

The fact that designers feel legitimate only in the event of political victory constitutes a setback for the field in many ways. Firstly because the role of designers in the war room (or, more broadly, in electoral communication processes) is still largely unexplored, and therefore the lack of debates that go beyond praise or condemnation in this context prevents the design discourse from progressing in any way in the field of design *with* politics. And secondly because, through a deterministic view of the political landscape, it becomes impossible to engage in dialogue with the Superstorm, which is instead a conglomeration of diverse forces that require an insightful and highly contextualized analysis of the social, political, geographical and technological context in which they operate.

In this kind of scenario, a re-discussion of the notion of mediation within the design field seems necessary as well. The issue of mediation is inevitably linked to the identification of the actors in today's political environment, which could translate into the question of: mediation between whom? In fact, whereas in the

1960s the political landscape was marked by a clear distinction between party and electorate, proletarian and industrial world, state and citizen, this divide has begun to disintegrate in a plethora of fragmentary and heterogeneous constellations. Today, political communication and the Western political sphere as a whole are characterized by a progressive disintegration that sees the weakening of the party in favor of the leader, the ability of voters to constitute political parties starting from virtual networking resources, and the possibility for citizens to actively participate in the creation of the online political visual culture, while the State (defined as a community's political and judicial organization) is increasingly perceived as a fictitious and absent entity. In this context, the position of designers as mediators between political organs and citizens is not only illusory, but also frequently ineffective.

However, as seen in chapter two, the contemporary political landscape is dominated by a slew of other mediating agents spawned by the introduction of new media technologies into the political sphere (including algorithms, politicians, and citizens themselves), which demand close scrutiny. In this sense, if the role of designers within this field cannot be that of 'active' mediators, they might serve as meta-mediators. This means that designers might not necessarily allow communication between party and citizens, but could and should examine the numerous mediating mechanisms put in place by the Superstorm and report them to the public through visualization processes.

As much as agency and mediation, the issue of authorship is also becoming increasingly complex. On the one hand, authorship carries with it a quest for legitimacy of the work of designers, the recognition of their role within society, and the hunger for affirmation. But on the other hand, this issue often leads to a more complicated debate over the issue of financial recognition of designers' work (if one considers recent debates over NFTs, for example, it is clear that the difficulty of recognizing the uniqueness of one's own work in the field of digital media is quite real and definitely still unexplored). Throughout the book, it has been established that the issue of authorship is not just limited to the need for affirmation in a given field, but also includes a broader system related to the need for designers to sustain their own work on a financial level. However, it is necessary to highlight the wilful blindness that many designers appear to have towards the systems within which political messages are being constructed across Western societies.

As seen in the category of design *of* politics, the Western contemporary political landscape is made up of a large number of actors who arise within the Superstorm and who operate 'intrinsically' to politics. 'Intrinsically' refers here to the modalities of producing, sharing, and reading images that are determined by the natural progression of the Superstorm, in which the process of mediatization introduced by new media technologies allows political communication to expand its possibilities for the creation and dissemination of political messages. In fact, the hyper-professionalization of political communication, as well as the ever-increasing availability of image creation tools, in conjunction with SNS, has enabled politicians as well as prosumers to create extraordinary political imaginaries that are far beyond the traditional representations of a candidate's body or political ideals.

If on one hand the communication created for politicians by their political strategists is based on the representation of an idealized view of society, on the other hand, citizens-users may contribute to bolster or demolish these imaginaries through the creation of fandom pages, memes, and other visual means made available by digital tools. These two actors, who are part of a much larger group of people who contribute to the Western political visual culture, have shown to be major players in the dissemination of political imaginaries and, as a result, deserve the attention of designers who want to interact with the Superstorm. It must be said, unfortunately, that because of the extreme confidentiality of the work performed by political strategists as well as the volatility that pervades grassroots internet-based image creation, these two fields may often appear impenetrable to designers. However, the recognition of these events in the first place, and their effects in the second, are both activities that could fall within the scope of design just as much as they fall within the scope of sociology and political theory since both fields (albeit with very different tools) can contribute to a better understanding of the processes that make up the political discourse.

To understand how designers might act within the context of Western political visual culture, it is necessary to abandon a number of preconceptions that clearly still exist about the relationship between designers and political communication. As seen throughout the book, it often appears that designers feel empowered to act only through design approaches that have already been extensively explored – such as the collaboration with a politician or party, or the use of the museum as a space for debate and confrontation. However, as shown in the third and last chapter, these approaches may end up excluding a significant amount of new possibilities for action, which include political communication phenomena that emerge spontaneously inside the Superstorm.

If read through the historical and critical lenses proposed by this study, this deliberate omission may be seen as the result of a series of coincidences and events that led designers to forego a more precise understanding of how to act in political processes. This point is masterfully expressed by German architect and writer Markus Miessen, who in his book *The Nightmare of Participation* claims defiantly that "in order to develop strategies for a post-nostalgic practice, one needs to get beyond the truism that in order to act fully democratic, everyone needs to be involved". Despite being written within the context of architectural practices, Miessen touches upon a fundamental issue about all aspects of the field of design (including communication design) that have to do with the notion of participation intended as the inclusion of all parts of society at all costs.

If one considers the first chapter of the book, set between the 1960s and early 1970s, it is quite easy to notice how certain design approaches might have left an indelible mark on the discourse of design as of how to engage citizens in the democratic process – the consequences of which are still visible today. The use of posters in an era dominated by television, the hopes placed on new media technologies as tools for liberation from state oppression, and the intellectual proximity with post-structuralist theories took place more than sixty years ago. Despite this, they fostered the idea that political participation could only be achieved via radical design approaches, through the physical presence of artifacts in cities' streets and squares, and fed by the total and ideological rejection of certain kinds of media.

Today, just as in the 1960s, the issue of participation is still fundamentally linked to understanding the forces that dominate the construction of the political scene. However, if one considers the category of design *of* politics, it can be observed how the agents who operate within the Superstorm today are proceeding and acting at a far faster rate than communication designers appear to be. This speed, which has proved to be a determining factor in the Superstorm, contrasts with an apparent fossilization within the field of communication design, which has a desire to involve 'everyone' in the political process while failing to understand (or refusing to see) the forces that surround it. About this, Miessen writes that

> "In a field of forces, it is the individual vectors that participate in its becoming. However, if one wants to participate in any given force field, it is crucial to identify the conflicting forces at

> play. In this context, 'participation' is not to be understood as the default form that promotes participatory planning processes or user-involvement, but as a means of a consciously directed, forced entry into a territory, system, discourse, or practice that one is not usually part of"[203].

The point highlighted by Miessen is critical for understanding the second aspect of post-nostalgic practices, which have to do with the fact that, over the years, communication designers have contributed to shape a specific idea (and usage) of different kinds of media.

As previously stated, a series of events from the 1960s and onwards led designers to reject the world of traditional media (such as radio and television), and to approach that of new media with a utopian slant, echoing the demands of cyber-cultures and promoting the idea of a world capable of transforming and improving itself through digital technologies. However, as British artist and writer James Bridle recalls in his book *New Dark Age*, the promise of a transformative and liberating network has turned in recent decades into a darkening reality, dictated by the weaponization of information and an unimaginable level of complexity. And, as Bridle writes:

> "If we do not understand how complex technologies function then their potential is more easily captured by selfish elites and corporations. The results of this can be seen all around us. There is a causal relationship between the complex opacity of the systems we encounter every day and

[203] M. MIESSEN, ED., *The Nightmare of Participation: (Crossbench Praxis as a Mode of Criticality)* (Cambridge, MA: Sternberg Press, 2011), 53.

> global issues of inequality, violence, populism and fundamentalism"[204].

In the same way, understanding and recounting the Superstorm is necessary in order to figure out how to weather it. And more specifically, because the Superstorm builds upon communication processes, designers have the intellectual ability and skill to achieve this task. However, in order to do so, they must first go through a critical re-examination of their history within the field of political communication, and begin to broaden or change their understanding of design processes, participation, and media – eschewing old myths and ideologies in favor of new and unexpected design approaches.

The first step in this direction might be to stop delegitimizing new media technologies in favor of traditional ones, and pay more attention to certain elements of our political visual culture that are the byproduct of it. The mockery of Trump's hat, the consideration of memes as 'funny' visual jokes, the lack of attention towards *la Bestia*: all these aspects can be considered as signs of a incomprehension towards the Superstorm, which meanwhile grows amongst laughter through gritted teeth, touches of screens, and the release of one's data amidst general tacit consent.

WEATHERING THE SUPERSTORM

As I mentioned earlier, the intention of this book is not to provide a navigation manual for the Superstorm, nor to state what designers can or cannot do in order to overcome it. However, in this final part of the book I will try to outline a series of

---

[204] J. BRIDLE, *New Dark Age: Technology and the End of the Future* (London: Verso Books, 2019), 9.

reflections on the attitude that designers can take with regard to the Superstorm, and which hopefully will be further developed or disproved by other scholars and practitioners dealing with these topics. These notes are clearly not intended as a *diktat*, but rather as an attempt to expose the considerations that this research has prompted during its development.

Firstly, throughout the book, it often appears that communication designers might have developed a conflict-laden relationship with their past, which can often get in their way of understanding the forces at play in the Superstorm. However, this friction is not ascribable to a deliberate choice of action; on the contrary, the stalemate could possibly be generated by an incomprehension of the development that new media technologies underwent from the 1960s until today. In this sense, the first step to weather the Superstorm is to critically interpret the traces left by the past debates over the relationship between new media and design practice, and embrace the awareness that the ever-changing notion of new media will give life to conditions that are always new and unpredicted, but that should be nonetheless acknowledged.

In the sprawling and omnivorous present dictated by the Superstorm, the experiences of the past can serve as an essential and critical tool for deciphering the current categories of design action, as well as the media landscape that surrounds them – but should never cause a setback. Through a more flexible interpretation of their role within society, designers acquire the intellectual ability to not only develop an historical understanding of our reality, but also of the technologies that are put into play within the Superstorm. This translates to the necessity to pay close attention to the tools with which our current mediatized political visual culture is designed and conceived. In order to do this, communication designers need to be aware of the different ways in which technology is put into use within the creation of political imaginaries, and mold their tools constantly in order to adapt to the changing landscape around them.

As a result of these considerations, the question that naturally arises is what role design will (or could) play in the future of the Superstorm. Clearly, the difficulty that designers have demonstrated in legitimizing the evolution of new media unveils a crisis in the relationships that design discourse has not only with history, but above all with technology.

In fact, the development of new media, starting from the 1960s, marked an increasing estrangement of design discourse from technologies, creating a gap that seems yet to be filled. Time after time, project after project, designers confirm or deny this relationship, which nonetheless appears to be the pivotal issue at the heart of designers' stalemate in the face of the Superstorm. Astray and without clear future coordinates, designers await a new language and a new mastery of technology – today no longer solely in their hands. Accepting the political, social, and economic decentralization of designers' position within the Superstorm represents probably the first step for a redefinition of the relationship between technology and design practice. The directions presented in this book – from the new authorial geographies to the new territories of design's social aspiration – all reside in the effort for a new awareness.

If designers are dealing with an entity that is constantly evolving, so must their practice be. This does not mean that they should erase what has been done in the past with regard to the Superstorm. On the contrary, as mentioned earlier, their past could and should be used in order to produce new and informed analytical systems to face our current and future political landscape. However, the planning of our future should not be held back by the disillusionment with the present and the longing for the past; in a present locked in the contingent, there is no space for the future.

Well aware that this book does not offer solutions nor 'operational' strategies to face the Superstorm, I would like to invite readers to reflect on the landscape that this study has outlined.

In fact, although the outcomes presented within the book do not provide immediate directions, the points made throughout the conclusions of each chapter have the aim to stimulate processes of re-discussion of the discourse of design and its coordinates within the context of the Superstorm.

As opposed to a manual, as mentioned in the initial remarks, this book does not foresee forms of control over the Superstorm, but rather contains a series of points which could lead design discourse to undertake a path of self-analysis. In this sense, I do not assume there is a reality awaiting discovery which can be excavated, nor that I have finally arrived at some sort of 'truth'. Nonetheless, what I would like to emphasize with this study is that between political realities and their visual representations there is a process of knowledge construction which passes through communicative artifacts that are partial, complex, and have resulted from a specific social and historical context. As a result, we can assume that the stalemate between design discourse and political communication can only be overcome if designers acknowledge all the social and political complexities that surround the production and dissemination of communicative artifacts – whether produced by designers or not – and bring them within design discourse. For these reasons, I believe that the formulation of a historical-critical research that stems from the point of view of design culture is necessary in order to comprehend the reasons which have led certain agencies to prevail over others, and for design to choose certain battlegrounds in comparison to others.

Overall, I hope that this book proves to be the first step of a wider research project, the intention of which is to build a legacy capable of stimulating a continuous debate around the central themes of contemporary politics and its representations through the lenses of design culture. Only by focusing on these points will it be possible, hopefully, to set sail and face the Superstorm – advancing into hitherto unexplored territories, and expanding the horizons of design discourse.

AUTHOR'S NOTE

The content of this book is an elaboration of my doctoral research conducted at Iuav University of Venice in the Design Science curriculum between 2018 and 2022. However, it would be restrictive to perimeter this research only to a scholarly endeavor. As a matter of fact, it is more accurate to frame the content of the book as the concluding and final stage of a longer and more heterogeneous path, which includes episodes of academic research as well as design projects. Over the last eight years, two different degree projects (one obtained at Free University of Bozen-Bolzano in 2016 and the other at Design Academy Eindhoven in 2018) allowed me to approach the topics treated in this book, providing an initial set of case studies related to intersection of design, politics and new media technologies.

During my doctoral research, I have had the opportunity to expand some of my research topics in articles published for magazines and journals, together with conferences and seminars which were undoubtedly influential in shaping my research approach and critiquing my results. Furthermore, the exhibition series GEO—DESIGN curated by Martina Muzi provided me with the opportunity to develop a short video-essay analyzing the events that occurred within the Italian political scene during the emergency caused by Covid-19 – a project which proved extremely useful to finalizing my research. And lastly, the seminar 'In Great Tempest' organized with Pierfrancesco Califano at Iuav University of Venice in June 2022 was a pivotal moment for the development of my thesis; firstly, because it represented a chance to deepen the existing discourse on the relationship between politics and design with the invited guests and the present strudents; but more importantly, it is this conference to which I owe the name of this book – resulting from the insight of Pierfrancesco who, while we were researching the name of the conference, quoted Dante's passage containing the words about the "great tempest". A tempest that, in the following months, evolved into the key metaphor of this book.

The dual and complementary nature of this book points back to what I believe to be the great protagonist of these pages (and this research more in general): the relationship between history and design, between theory and practice. What happens between political communication and communication design is just one of the many scenarios in which the design discourse manifests its positions and fragilities in the face of societal events, in a climax of contradictions and complexities that are summarized here through the metaphor of the Superstorm. Investigating this specific relationship brings out not only how designers situate themselves within society, but more importantly what idea of society is brought forward by the design practice. The hybrid approach between design and research that characterizes this work has exposed questions that cannot possibly be answered in a single book, and that I hope will be further explored in the future by researchers with similar interests.

Nevertheless, the historical events chronicled here recount a new confidence in the reading of modern design history, where the aim is not to understand the mistakes of the past, but rather to find new questions to investigate it.

INDEX OF NAMES

ADORNO, T. W. 44, 89, 90
AIELLO, G. 45
ALI, M. 71–73
ALTHEIDE, D. L. 85
ANDERSON, B. R. O. 182
ARENDT, H. 100
ARMANO, E. 90–92, 144
ARPA; 45, 47, 53
ATELIER POPULAIRE; 12, 58–62, 66, 69

BANNON, S. K. 157-165
BARTHES, R. 117
BASSETTI, C. 92
BAUDRILLARD, J. 85, 88–90, 141
BEAN, C. 113
BEIFUSS, A. 19
BENJAMIN, W. 89, 119
BENNETT, W. L. 111, 112, 115
BEST, S. 91
BIERUT, M. 11, 145, 147–150, 152, 190, 191, 193
BILLARD, T. J. 147
BLOOMBERG, M. 17
BLUMLER, J. G. 166
BONSIEPE, G. 57
BOORSTIN, D. J. 87–90, 102
BORRELLI, A. 177
BOUVIER, J. 40
BREXIT; 16, 18, 150, 198
BRIDLE, J. 206, 207
BRIZIARELLI, M. 90–92, 144
BROUGH, M. M. 181
BURNETT, M. 143
BUSH, G. H. W. 133

CAMBRIDGE ANALYTICA; 151–153
CASAPOUND; 170

CASTELLS, M. 28
CHELES, L. 64, 66–68
CHIN, B. 182
CLINTON, H. 132, 134, 145, 147, 150–154, 190, 191, 200, 201
CONSIDINE, L. 59, 61
CONTE, G. 177–188
CONWAY, K. 126
COSENZA, G. 55
COSGROVE, K. 151
COULDRY, N. 85
COVID-19; 17, 177
CRANBROOK ACADEMY OF ART; 116
CROUCH, C. 127, 128
CROW, D. A. 187

DANTE, A. 12, 21, 22
DAYAN, D. 100–104.
DC; 66, 67
DE ROUGEMONT, G. 59
DEBORD, G. 45, 61, 74, 80, 88, 90, 92, 98, 99, 121
DESIGN OBSERVER; 149
DETTI, T. 47
DI MAIO, L. 179, 188
DICHTER, E. 66, 67
DISALVO, C. 97, 99
DREW, R. 40, 43
DUNNE, A. 96

ÉCOLE DES BEAUX-ARTS; 58, 59
EISENHOWER, D.D. 36, 38, 39, 68
EMIGRE; 118
ENTMAN, R. M. 187
ERIKSON, E. 180
ESSER, F. 84
ESQUIRE; 71–73
EYE MAGAZINE; 117

INDEX OF NAMES

FACEBOOK; 104, 135, 136, 140, 170, 172–175, 179, 180, 183–185, 188
FAIREY, S. 138
FALLAN, K. 109
FARAGE, N. 198
FAST COMPANY; 152
FELSENSTEIN, L. 53
FISCHER, C. 71
FIVE STAR MOVEMENT; 179
FLAKE, E. 146
FLICHY, P. 54
FORD, P. 145
FOUCAULT, M. 117
FRANKFURT, S. O. 69, 70
FRATELLI D'ITALIA; 179, 188
FRY, T. 99, 100
FULLER, B. 82

GARLAND, K. 56
GERVEREAU, L. 59
GHEBREYESUS, T. A. 177
GOFFMAN, E. 187
GOLDING, W. 21, 22
GUNSTER, S. 178

HABERMAS, J. 44, 45, 85
HARNWELL, B. 157
HAUSER, S. 106
HEADRICK, B. 113
HEGEDUS, C. 133
HELLER, S. 19, 35, 118, 147
HENDERSON, H. 47
HEPP, A. 85
HET NIEUWE INSTITUUT; 159, 162, 191
HJARVARD, S. 85
HONEYWELL; 47
HORKHEIMER, M. 44, 89, 90
HUGES, C. 136

IBM; 47
IHDE, D. 107
ILLICH, I. 47, 82

INGOLD, T. 108
INNIS, H. 27
INSTAGRAM; 16–18, 104, 174, 188, 198

JONES, B. 150
JULIER, G. 23, 24, 26, 27, 31
KATZ, E. 101–103
KAVANAGH, D. 166
KAY, A. 47
KELLNER, D. 91
KELLY, V. 24
KENNEDY, J. F. 36–40, 43, 46, 53, 68, 73, 78, 80, 100
KINON, J. 152, 153
KOZLOV, C. 74
KRIPPENDORFF, K. 25, 26
KROTZ, F. 85

LA BESTIA; 166, 167, 169, 172–176, 192, 193, 207
LABARRE, S. 152, 153
LANOUE, D. J. 113
LAURETANO, M. 76, 78
LAWLOR, A. 187
LA7; 171
LE BIMBE DI GIUSEPPE CONTE; 180, 182, 184, 188, 194, 199
LE PEN, M. 167, 168
LEES-MAFFEI, G. 109, 110
LEGA; 166–170, 176, 178, 188
LEVY, P. 182
LICKLIDER, J. C. R. 47, 48, 50
LICKO, Z. 118
LIFE MAGAZINE; 40–42
LINDSAY, J. 70
LIPKIN, E. 51
LOIS, G. 69, 73
LUPTON, E. 119

MAD MEN; 152–155
MAGNO, B. 64, 65
MALDONADO, T. 56
MAMBER, S. 43

MANIN, B. 128
MANOVICH, L. 55
MARCUSE, H. 90
MARTIN, B. 153
MAULDIN, P. 148
MAYER, P. A. 48
MCALLISTER, I. 112, 113
MCCARTHY, J. 57, 74, 75, 76
MCLUHAN, M. 27, 37, 47, 82, 83, 89
MCCOY, K. 116
MCSHINE, K. 74, 76, 77
MCQUISTON, L. 17
MELONI, G. 179, 188
MEYER, M. 184
MIESSEN, M. 204–206
MODES OF CRITICISM; 198
MOMA; 74, 80
MONTOYA, M. 60
MORIMOTO, L. H. 182
MORISI, L. 167, 171, 176, 193
MOUFFE, C. 97, 98
MOVIMENTO 5 STELLE; 179, 188
MUGHAN, A. 113
MUNCH, A. V. 26, 31
MURGIA, A. 92

NBC; 126, 143
N.E. THING CO. 74
NELSON, T. H. 47, 49–51
NEW YORKER; 145, 146
NIX, A. 153, 154
NIXON, R. M. 36, 37, 38, 40, 43, 46, 53, 61, 73, 78, 100
NORRIS, P. 103, 104, 133, 134
NOSSITER, T. J. 166

OBAMA, B. 12, 126, 127, 134–142, 145, 147, 190, 194, 200
OLIVETTI; 75
ONG, W. J. 27, 130
OOGJES, D. 106
ORTF; 61
OTERO VERZIER, M. 159, 162–165, 192

PARC; 47
PAPANEK, V. 56, 57
PARRY, K. 45
PATTERSON, T. E. 114
PCI; 64, 65
PELLICANI, M. 68
PENCE, M. 149
PENNEBAKER, D. A. 133
PINOTTI, A. 83, 84
PLOUFFE, D. 134, 135
PORNHUB; 185, 186
POSTER, M. 54
PRI; 64, 65
PSI; 64, 65

RABY, F. 96
REEVES, R. 38
REEVES-EVISON, T. 96
ROCK, M. 117, 118
ROSPARS, J. 135

SALA, G. 179
SALVINI, M. 167–175, 179, 188
SAMUELSOHN, D. 147
SANDVOSS, C. 181, 182
SAURETTE, P. 178
SCAMMELL, M. 166
SCHWEIZER, P. 160
SEGERBERG, A. 115
SENDER LLC; 135
SENDER, S. 145
SHAKESPEARE, W. 21, 22
SHANNON, C. 53
SHAW, J. K. 96
SHILS, E. 101
SHRESTHOVA, S. 181
SLABYK, J. 135, 136
SOLLAZZO, L. 68
SOMAINI, A. 83, 84
SONTAG, S. 184
SORENSEN, T. 37
SOTTSASS, E. 75
SNOW, R. P. 85
SPANKY AND OUR GANG; 70

SPERA, M. 64, 65
SPICER, S. 126
SUTHERLAND, I. 47
STAAL, J. 158–165, 192
STANFORD UNIVERSITY; 47
STRÖMBÄCK, J. 85
SZPAKOWSKI, M. 51

TAGGART, P. 163, 164
TANK SINATRA, @; 18
TAYLOR, R. W. 47, 48
TEDESCHI, R. 67
TELI, M. 92
THE APPRENTICE; 143, 151
THE MOVEMENT; 157
THOMAS, S. 134–136, 137, 139, 141, 142, 147, 190, 193, 194
TILLMANS, W. 18
TIME MAGAZINE; 40–42
TODD, C. 126
TRAGANOU, J. 19
TRIVINI BELLINI, F. 19
TRUMP, D. 17, 126, 127, 143–145, 149–154, 157–161, 163, 166, 169, 185, 191, 192, 198, 207
TURNER, F. 49, 101
TWITTER; 104, 144, 145, 148, 149, 174, 198

UC BERKELEY; 47
UC SANTA BARBARA; 47
ULM SCHOOL OF DESIGN; 57
URBINATI, N. 128, 129
U.U.U. 58

VAN ZOONEN, L. 181
VANDERLANS, R. 118
VERBEEK, P.-P. 106–108, 110
VITALE, E. 64, 65

WAKKARY, R. 106
WALKER, J. A. 109
WATSON, A. 43
WATTPAD; 185, 186

WEAVER, W. 53
WEINGARD, W. 116
WIEGAND, P. 145
WILLSHER, K. 168
WIKILEAKS; 145, 146
WOLFF, R. 148, 149

XEROX; 47

YOUTUBE; 104, 135, 165, 174, 185, 186

ZAVATTARO, S. M. 140, 141

BIBLIOGRAPHY

INTRODUCTION

Beifuss, Artur, Francesco Trivini Bellini, and Steven Heller. *Branding Terror: The Logotypes and Iconography of Insurgent Groups and Terrorist Organizations*. London: Merrell Publishers, 2013.

Castells, Manuel. *End of Millennium*. Oxford: Blackwell Publishers, 1998.

———. *The Power of Identity*. Oxford: Blackwell Publishing, 1997.

———. *The Rise of the Network Society*. Oxford: Blackwell Publishing, 1996.

Julier, Guy. *The Culture of Design*. London: SAGE, 2000.

Julier, Guy, and Anders V. Munch. "Introducing Design Culture." In *Design Culture: Objects and Approaches*, edited by Guy Julier, Anders V. Munch, Mads Nygaard Folkmann, Hans-Christian Jensen, and Niels Peter Skou, 1–7. London: Bloomsbury Publishing, 2019.

Kelly, Veronika. "Culture, Practice, Discourse: A Theoretical Framework for a Critical Approach to Communication Design." *Studies in Material Thinking* 15, NO. 4 (2016): 1–17.

Krippendorff, Klaus. "Design Discourse." In *Design Discourse*, 333–41. Bielefeld: transcript Verlag, 2021.

Innis, Harold Adams. *Empire and Communications*. Lanham, MD: Rowman & Littlefield, 2007.

Manovich, Lev. *Software Culture*. Milano: Edizioni Olivares, 2010.

McLuhan, Marshall. *The Gutenberg Galaxy: The Making of Typographic Man*. Toronto: University of Toronto Press, 1962.

———. *Understanding Media: The Extensions of Man*. New York: McGraw-Hill, 1964.

McQuiston, Liz. *Graphic Agitation. Social and Political Graphics since the Sixties*. New York, NY: Phaidon, 2006.

———. *Visual Impact: Creative Dissent in the 21st Century*. London: Phaidon, 2015.

Ong, Walter J. *Orality and Literacy: The Technologizing of the Word*. London: Methuen, 1982.

Traganou, Jilly, ed. *Design and Political Dissent: Spaces, Visuals, Materialities*. New York: Routledge, 2020.

I
GENEALOGY OF THE SUPERSTORM.
NEW MEDIA, POLITICS, AND DESIGN

Aiello, Giorgia, and Katy Parry. "Aesthetics, Political." In *The International Encyclopedia of Political Communication*, 1–5. American Cancer Society, 2016.

———. *Visual Communication: Understanding Images in Media Culture*. London: SAGE, 2019.

Cheles, Luciano. "Picture battles in the piazza: the political poster." In *The Art of Persuasion: Political Communication in Italy from 1945 to the 1990s*, edited by Luciano Cheles and Lucio Sponza, 124–78. Manchester: Manchester University Press, 2001.

Cheles, Luciano, and Lucio Sponza, eds. *The Art of Persuasion: Political Communication in Italy from 1945 to the 1990s*. Manchester: Manchester University Press, 2001.

Considine, Liam. "Screen Politics: Pop Art and the Atelier Populaire – Tate Papers." *Tate Papers*, NO. 24 (Autumn 2015). https://www.tate.org.uk/research/publications/tate-papers/24/screen-politics-pop-art-and-the-atelier-populaire.

Cosenza, Giovanna. *Introduzione alla semiotica dei nuovi media*. Bari: Editori Laterza, 2014.

———. *Semiotica e comunicazione politica*. Bari: Editori Laterza, 2018.

Debord, Guy. *Comments on the Society of the Spectacle*. London: Verso, 1998.

———. *The Society of the Spectacle*. Detroit: Black and Red, 1967.

Detti Tommaso. "Joseph C. R. Licklider e le origini di Internet: tecnica, ricerca scientifica e società." *PC*, 2014, 167–76.

Flichy, Patrice. *The Internet Imaginaire*. Cambridge, MA: MIT Press, 2007.

Gervereau, Laurent. "Les affiches de 'mai 68.'" *Matériaux pour l'histoire de notre temps* 11, NO. 1 (1988): 160–71.

Habermas, Jürgen. *Strukturwandel Der Öffentlichkeit: Untersuchungen Zu Einer Kategorie Der Bürgerlichen Gesellschaft*. Frankfurt: Suhrkamp Verlag, 1962.

———. *The Theory of Communicative Action, Volume 1: Reason and the Rationalization of Society*. Boston: Beacon Press, 1984.

———. *The Theory of Communicative Action, Volume 2: Lifeworld and System: A Critique of Functionalist Reason*. Boston: Beacon Press, 1988.

Heller, Steven. *Iron Fists. Branding the 20th-century totalitarian state*. New York: Phaidon, 2008.

Horkheimer, Max, and Theodor W. Adorno. *Dialektik Der Aufklärung*. Amsterdam: Querido, 1947.

Henderson, Harry. *Communications and Broadcasting: From Wired Words to Wireless Web*. New York: Infobase Publishing, 2007.

Katz, Elihu, and Paul Felix Lazarsfeld. *Personal Influence: The Part Played by People in the Flow of Mass*. New York: The Free Press, 1955.

Kraus, Sidney. *Televised Presidential Debates and Public Policy*. Mahwah: Lawrence Erlbaum Associates, 1988.

———. *The Great Debates: Background, Perspective, Effects*. Bloomington: Indiana University Press, 1962.

Licklider, Joseph Carl Robnett, and Robert W. Taylor. "The Computer as a Communication Device." *Science and Technology*, 1968.

Mamber, Stephen. *Cinema Verite in America: Studies In Uncontrolled Documentary*. Cambridge: MIT Press, 1974.

Manovich, Lev. *The Language of New Media*. Cambridge, MA: MIT Press, 2001.

Mayer, Paul A. *Computer Media and Communication: A Reader*. Oxford: Oxford University Press, 1999.

McCarthy, Jeremiah William. "The Artist and the 'Information' Machine: Conceptualism, Technology, and Design in 1970." CUNY Hunter College, 2016.

McLuhan, Marshall. *Understanding Media: The Extensions of Man*. New York: McGraw-Hill, 1964.

Natchez, Peter B. *Images of Voting - Visions of Democracy*. Piscataway: Transaction Publishers, 1985.

Nelson, Theodor H. *Computer Lib: You Can and Must Understand*

Computers NOW / Dream Machines: New Freedoms Through Computer Screens — a Minority Report. Chicago: Self-published, 1974.

O'Connell, P. J. *Robert Drew and the Development of Cinema Verite in America*. Carbondale: Southern Illinois University Press, 2010.

Poster, Mark. *What's the Matter with the Internet?* Minneapolis: University Of Minnesota Press, 2001.

Sollazzo, Lucia. "Pubblicità Elettorale." *Sipradue*, December 1968.

Turner, Fred. *From Counterculture to Cyberculture: Stewart Brand, the Whole Earth Network, and the Rise of Digital Utopianism*. Chicago: The University of Chicago Press, 2006.

U.U.U. *L'atelier populaire présenté par lui-même*. Self-published, 1968.

II
ANATOMY OF THE SUPERSTORM.
DESIGN ISSUES IN A MEDIATIZED WORLD

Adam, Silke, and Michaela Maier. "Personalization of Politics A Critical Review and Agenda for Research." *Annals of the International Communication Association* 34, NO. 1 (January 1, 2010): 213–57.

Altheide, David L. "Media Logic." In *The International Encyclopedia of Political Communication*, 1–6. American Cancer Society, 2016.

Altheide, David L., and Robert P. Snow. "Toward a Theory of Mediation." *Annals of the International Communication Association* 11, NO. 1 (January 1, 1988): 194–223.

Arendt, Hannah. *The Life of the Mind*. New York: Harcourt, Brace & Co., 1978.

Barthes, Roland. "The Death of the Author." In *Image Music Text*, 142–48. New York: Fontana Press, 1977.

Bassetti, Chiara, Annalisa Murgia, and Maurizio Teli. "Tin Hat Games – Producing, Funding, and Consuming an Independent Role-Playing Game in the Age of the Interactive Spectacle." In *The Spectacle 2.0: Reading Debord in the Context of Digital Capitalism*, edited by Marco Briziarelli and Emiliana Armano, 167–82. London:

University of Westminster Press, 2017.

Baudrillard, Jean. *For a Critique of the Political Economy of the Sign.* Candor: Telos Press, 1981.

———. *In the Shadow of the Silent Majorities: Or, The End of the Social and Other Essays.* Cambridge, MA: Semiotext(e), 1983.

———. *Simulacra and Simulation.* Ann Arbor: University of Michigan Press, 1994.

———. The Ecstasy of Communication. Translated by Bernard Schütze and Caroline Schütze. New York: Semiotext(e), 1987.

Bean, Clive, and Anthony Mughan. "Leadership Effects in Parliamentary Elections in Australia and Britain." *American Political Science Review* 83, NO. 4 (December 1989): 1165–79.

Benjamin, Walter. "The Author as Producer." In *Understanding Brecht*, 85–103. London; New York: Verso, 1998.

Bennett, W. Lance. *The Logic of Connective Action: Digital Media And The Personalization Of Contentious Politics.* Cambridge: Cambridge University Press, 2014.

———. "The Personalization of Politics: Political Identity, Social Media, and Changing Patterns of Participation." *The Annals of the American Academy of Political and Social Science* 644 (2012): 20–39.

Bennett, W. Lance, and Alexandra Segerberg. "Digital Media and the Personalization of Collective Action." *Information, Communication & Society* 14, NO. 6 (September 1, 2011): 770–99.

Best, Steven, and Douglas Kellner. "Debord, Cybersituations, and the Interactive Spectacle." *SubStance* 28, NO. 3 (1999): 129–56.

———. "Postmodern Politics and the Battle for the Future." *New Political Science* 20, NO. 3 (September 1, 1998): 283–99.

Boorstin, Daniel J. *The Image: A Guide to Pseudo-Events in America.* New York: Harper, 1962.

Briziarelli, Marco, and Emiliana Armano. "Introduction: From the Notion of Spectacle to Spectacle 2.0: The Dialectic of Capitalist Mediations." In *The Spectacle 2.0: Reading Debord in the Context of Digital Capitalism*, edited by Marco Briziarelli and Emiliana Armano, 15–47. London: University of Westminster Press, 2017.

Brydon, Steven, Susan A. Hellweg, and Michael Pfau. *Televised Presidential Debates: Advocacy in Contemporary America*. New York: Praeger, 1992.

Campus, Donatella. "Mediatization and Personalization of Politics in Italy and France: The Cases of Berlusconi and Sarkozy." *The International Journal of Press/Politics* 15, NO. 2 (April 1, 2010): 219–35.

Caprara, Gian Vittorio. "The Personalization of Modern Politics." *European Review* 15, NO. 2 (May 2007): 151–64.

Couldry, Nick, Andreas Hepp, and Friedrich Krotz. *Media Events in a Global Age*. Abingdon: Routledge, 2009.

Dayan, Daniel, and Elihu Katz. Media Events: The Live Broadcasting of History. Cambridge, MA: Harvard University Press, 1992.

DiSalvo, Carl. *Adversarial Design*. Cambridge, MA: MIT Press, 2015.

Dunne, Anthony, and Fiona Raby. *Speculative Everything: Design, Fiction, and Social Dreaming*. Cambridge, MA: MIT Press, 2013.

Esser, Frank. "Mediatization as a Challenge: Media Logic Versus Political Logic." In *Democracy in the Age of Globalization and Mediatization*, edited by Hanspeter Kriesi, Sandra Lavenex, Frank Esser, Jörg Matthes, Marc Bühlmann, and Daniel Bochsler, 155–76. Challenges to Democracy in the 21st Century Series. London: Palgrave Macmillan UK, 2013.

Fallan, Kjetil. "De-Scribing Design: Appropriating Script Analysis to Design History." *Design Issues* 24, NO. 4 (October 1, 2008): 61–75.

Foucault, Michel. "What Is an Author?" In *Aesthetics, Method, and Epistemology*, edited by James D. Faubion, translated by Robert Hurley, 205–22. New York: The New Press, 1999.

Fry, Tony. *A New Design Philosophy: An Introduction to Defuturing*. Sydney: UNSW Press, 1999.

———. *Defuturing: A New Design Philosophy*. London: Bloomsbury Visual Arts, 2020.

———. *Design as Politics*. Oxford: Berg Publishers, 2010.

Garzia, Diego. *Personalization of Politics and Electoral Change*. Houndmills, Basingstoke: Palgrave Macmillan, 2014.

———. "Personalization of Politics Between Television and the Internet: Leader Effects in the 2013 Italian Parliamentary Election." *Journal of Information Technology & Politics* 14, NO. 4 (October 2, 2017): 403–16.

Hjarvard, Stig. "The Mediatization of Society." *Nordicom Review* 29, NO. 2 (November 1, 2008): 102–31.

Horkheimer, Max, and Theodor W Adorno. *Dialectic of Enlightenment*. London: Allen Lane, 1973.

Ingold, Timothy. "Introduction: The Perception of the User-Producer." In *Design and Anthropology*, edited by Wendy Gunn and Jared Donovan, 19–33. Anthropological Studies on Creativity and Perception. Farnham: Ashgate Publishing, 2012.

Kaase, Max. "Is There Personalization in Politics? Candidates and Voting Behavior in Germany." *International Political Science Review / Revue Internationale de Science Politique* 15, NO. 3 (1994): 211–30.

Katz, Elihu. "Disintermediation: Cutting Out the Middle Man." *Intermedia* 16, NO. 2 (March 1, 1988): 30–31.

Katz, Elihu, and Daniel Dayan. "Contests, Conquests, Coronations: On Media Events and Their Heroes." In *Changing Conceptions of Leadership*, edited by Carl F. Graumann and Serge Moscovici, 135–44. Springer Series in Social Psychology. New York, NY: Springer, 1986.

———. "Media Events: On the Experience of Not Being There." *Religion* 15, NO. 3 (July 1, 1985): 305–14.

Katz, Elihu, Daniel Dayan, and Pierre Motyl. "Communications in the 21st Century: In Defense of Media Events." *Organizational Dynamics* 10, NO. 2 (Settembre 1981): 68–80.

Lanoue, David J., and Barbara Headrick. "Prime Ministers, Parties, and the Public: The Dynamics of Government Popularity in Great Britain." *The Public Opinion Quarterly* 58, NO. 2 (1994): 191–209.

Lees-Maffei, Grace. "The Production–Consumption–Mediation Paradigm." *Journal of Design History* 22, NO. 4 (December 1, 2009): 351–76.

Licko, Zuzana, and Rudy VanderLans. "Ambition/Fear." *Emigre*, 1989.

Lupton, Ellen. "The Designer as Producer." In *The Education of a Graphic Designer*, edited by Stephen Heller, 159–62. New York: Allworth Press, 1998.

Marcuse, Herbert. *One Dimensional Man: Studies in the Ideology of Advanced Industrial Society*. Boston: Beacon Press, 1964.

Mazzoleni, Gianpietro. "A Return to Civic and Political Engagement Prompted by Personalized Political Leadership?" *Political Communication* 17, NO. 4 (October 1, 2000): 325–28.

———. "Mediatization of Politics." In *The International Encyclopedia of Communication*. American Cancer Society, 2008.

Mazzoleni, Gianpietro, and Winfried Schulz. "'Mediatization' of Politics: A Challenge for Democracy?" *Political Communication* 16, NO. 3 (July 1, 1999): 247–61.

McAllister, Ian. "Prime Ministers, Opposition Leaders and Government Popularity in Australia." *Australian Journal of Political Science* 38, NO. 2 (July 1, 2003): 259–77.

———. "The Personalization of Politics." In *The Oxford Handbook of Political Behavior*, edited by Russell J. Dalton and Hans-Dieter Klingemann, 571–88. Oxford: Oxford University Press, 2007.

Mcquire, Scott. "Rethinking Media Events: Large Screens, Public Space Broadcasting and Beyond." *New Media & Society* 12, NO. 4 (Giugno 2010): 567–82.

Mitu, Bianca, and Stamatis Poulakidakos. *Media Events: A Critical Contemporary Approach*. Springer, 2016.

Mouffe, Chantal. *Agonistics: Thinking The World Politically*. London: Verso, 2013.

———. *The Democratic Paradox*. London: Verso, 2000.

———. *The Return of the Political*. London: Verso, 2005.

Musella, Fortunato. "The Personalization of Italian Political Parties in Three Acts." *Contemporary Italian Politics* 0, NO. 0 (October 26, 2020): 1–14.

Norris, Pippa. "The Evolution of Election Campaigns: Eroding Political Engagement?" St Margaret's College, University of Otago, New Zealand: University of Otago, 2004.

———, ed. "The Rise of the Postmodern Campaign?" In *A Virtuous Circle: Political Communications in Postindustrial Societies*, 162–80. Communication, Society and Politics. Cambridge, MA: Cambridge University Press, 2000.

Patterson, Thomas E. *Out of Order*. New York: Vintage Books, 1994.

Rock, Micheal. "The Designer as Author." *Eye* 5, NO. 20 (1996). https://2x4.org/ideas/1996/designer-as-author/.

Shaw, Jon K., and Theo Reeves-Evison, eds. *Fiction as Method*. Cambridge, MA: Sternberg Press, 2017.

Shils, Edward. *Center and Periphery: Essays in Macrosociology*. Chicago: University of Chicago Press, 1975.

Strömbäck, Jesper. "Four Phases of Mediatization: An Analysis of the Mediatization of Politics." *The International Journal of Press/Politics* 13, NO. 3 (July 1, 2008): 228–46.

Van Zoonen, Liesbet. "'Finally, I Have My Mother Back': Politicians and Their Families in Popular Culture." *Harvard International Journal of Press/Politics* 3, NO. 1 (January 1, 1998): 48–64.

Verbeek, Peter-Paul. "Introduction: Humanity in Design." In *Design and Anthropology*, edited by Wendy Gunn and Jared Donovan, 163–76. Anthropological Studies on Creativity and Perception. Farnham: Ashgate Publishing, 2012.

———. "Materializing Morality: Design Ethics and Technological Mediation." *Science, Technology, & Human Values* 31, NO. 3 (May 2006): 361–80.

Walker, John A. *Design History and the History of Design*. London: Pluto Press, 1990.

III
DESIGN AND THE SUPERSTORM.
DESIGN *WITH* / *ABOUT* / *OF* POLITICS

Anderson, Benedict. *Imagined Communities: Reflections on the Origin and Spread of Nationalism*. London: Verso Books, 1983.

Baudrillard, Jean. *For a Critique of the Political Economy of the Sign*.

Candor: Telos Press, 1981.

———. *Simulacra and Simulation*. Ann Arbor: University of Michigan Press, 1994.

———. *The Consumer Society: Myths and Structures*. Los Angeles: SAGE, 1998.

———. *The Ecstasy of Communication*. New York: Semiotext(e), 1987.

Bierut, Michael. "I'm With Her: What I Learned Designing a Logo for Hillary Clinton." *Design Observer* (blog), March 28, 2017.

Billard, Thomas J. "Citizen Typography and Political Brands in the 2016 US Presidential Election Campaign." SSRN Scholarly Paper. Rochester, NY: Social Science Research Network, March 15, 2018.

Blankenship, Christina M. "President, Wrestler, Spectacle: An Examination of Donald Trump's Firing Tweets and The Celebrity Appresident as Response to Trump's Media Landscape." *Journal of Communication Inquiry* 44, NO. 2 (April 1, 2020): 117–38.

Blumler, Jay G., Dennis Kavanagh, and T. J. Nossiter. "Modern Communications versus Traditional Politics in Britain: Unstable Marriage of Convenience." In *Politics, Media, and Modern Democracy: An International Study of Innovations in Electoral Campaigning and Their Consequences*, edited by Paolo Mancini and David L. Swanson, 49–72. Praeger Series in Political Communication. Westport, Conn: Praeger, 1996.

Bonsiepe, Gui. "A Step Towards the Reinvention of Graphic Design." *Design Issues* 10, NO. 1 (1994): 47–52.

Brandt, Stefan L. "Donald Trump, the Reality Show: Populism as Performance and Spectacle." *Zeitschrift Für Literaturwissenschaft Und Linguistik* 50, NO. 2 (June 1, 2020): 303–21.

Brough, Melissa M., and Sangita Shresthova. "Fandom Meets Activism: Rethinking Civic and Political Participation." *Transformative Works and Cultures* 10 (June 15, 2012).

Castells, Manuel. *Networks of Outrage and Hope: Social Movements in the Internet Age*. Hoboken, NJ: John Wiley & Sons, 2015.

Clarke, Isobelle, and Jack Grieve. "Stylistic Variation on the Donald Trump Twitter Account: A Linguistic Analysis of Tweets Posted between 2009 and 2018." *PLOS ONE* 14, NO. 9 (set 2019): e0222062.

Cosgrove, Ken. "The Emotional Brand Wins." edited by Anastasia Veneti, Darren Lilleker, Daniel Jackson, and Einar Thorsen, 27. Poole, UK: The Centre for the Study of Journalism, Culture and Community, 2016. http://www.ElectionAnalysis2016.US.

Crouch, Colin. *Coping with Post-Democracy.* London: Fabian Society, 2000.

Crow, Deserai A., and Andrea Lawlor. "Media in the Policy Process: Using Framing and Narratives to Understand Policy Influences." *Review of Policy Research* 33, NO. 5 (2016): 472–91.

Entman, Robert M. "Framing Bias: Media in the Distribution of Power." *Journal of Communication* 57, NO. 1 (2007): 163–73.

Erikson, Edward. "'Hillary Is My Friend': MySpace and Political Fandom." *Rocky Mountain Communication Review* 5, NO. 1 (2008): 3–16.

Ford, Paul. "The Emergence of Crowdsmashing Logos and Rebranding." *New York Magazine* (blog), December 21, 2012.

Fuchs, Christian. *Digital Demagogue: Authoritarian Capitalism in the Age of Trump and Twitter.* Pluto Press, 2018.

Goffman, Erving. *Frame Analysis: An Essay on the Organization of Experience.* Boston: Northeastern University Press, 1986.

Het Nieuwe Instituut. (2018, July 2). Steve Bannon: A Propaganda Retrospective | An exhibition project by Jonas Staal. Hetnieuweinstituut.Nl. https://steve-bannon-propaganda-retrospective.hetnieuweinstituut.nl

Howarth, Dan. "Trump May Have Won 'Not in Spite of His Terrible Design Work, but Because of It' Says Hillary Clinton's Logo Designer." *Dezeen* (blog), March 30, 2017. https://www.dezeen.com/2017/03/30/michael-bierut-pentagram-hillary-clinton-us-presidential-campaign-logo-design-concerns/.

In the Face of Evil: Reagan's War in Word and Deed. Documentary. Bannon Films, Leo McWatkins, Renegade Productions, 2004.

Jones, Barbara. "The MAGA Hat, a Curious Artifact of Contemporary

America." *Anthropology News* 60, NO. 4 (July 2019).

Kellner, Douglas. "Donald Trump and the Politics of the Spectacle." In *American Nightmare*, by Douglas Kellner, 3–6. Transgressions. Rotterdam: SensePublishers, 2016.

———. "Guy Debord, Donald Trump, and the Politics of the Spectacle." In *The Spectacle 2.0*, edited by Marco Briziarelli and Emiliana Armano, 5:1–14. Reading Debord in the Context of Digital Capitalism. University of Westminster Press, 2017.

———. "Trump's War Against the Media, Fake News, and (A)Social Media." In *Trump's Media War*, edited by Catherine Happer, Andrew Hoskins, and William Merrin, 47–67. Cham: Springer International Publishing, 2019.

Kinon, Jennifer, and Bobby Martin. Design Has A Huge Role To Play In Politics, Even If It Can't Win An Election. Interview by Suzanne LaBarre. Video, April 28, 2017. https://www.youtube.com/watch?v=Nk5cLZepyDQ.

Lee, Soobum, and Won-Ki Moon. "New Public Segmentation for Political Public Relations Using Political Fandom: Understanding Relationships between Individual Politicians and Fans." *Public Relations Review* 47, NO. 4 (November 1, 2021): 102084.

Levy, Pierre. *Collective Intelligence*. Cambridge: Basic Books, 1999.

Manin, Bernard. *The Principles of Representative Government. Themes in the Social Sciences.* Cambridge: Cambridge University Press, 1997.

Meyer, Moe. *The Politics and Poetics of Camp*. London: Psychology Press, 1994.

Morimoto, Lori Hitchcock, and Bertha Chin. "Reimagining the Imagined Community: Online Media Fandoms in the Age of Global Convergence." In *Fandom: Identities and Communities in a Mediated World*, edited by Jonathan Gray, Cornel Sandvoss, and C. Lee Harrington, 174–88. New York: NYU Press, 2017.

Nix, Alexander. "From Mad Men to Math Men." YouTube Video presented at the Online Marketing Rockstars Keynote | OMR17, Hamburg, Germany, March 10, 2017. https://www.youtube.com/watch?reload=9&v=6bG5ps5KdDo&ab_channel=OMR.

Norris, Pippa. "The Evolution of Election Campaigns: Eroding Political Engagement?" St Margaret's College, University of Otago, New Zealand: University of Otago, 2004.

Otero Verzier, Marina. "Propaganda at the Museum." In *Steve Bannon: A Propaganda Retrospective By Jonas Staal*, by Jonas Staal and Marina Otero Verzier, 5–9. Rotterdam: Het Nieuwe Instituut, 2018.

Pérez-Curiel, Concha, and Pilar Limón-Naharro. "Political Influencers. A Study of Donald Trump's Personal Brand on Twitter and Its Impact on the Media and Users." *Communication & Society*, 2019, 57–75.

Samuelsohn, Darren. "Design Experts Trash Hillary's New Logo." POLITICO (blog), April 17, 2015. https://www.politico.com/story/2015/04/design-experts-trash-hillary-clintons-new-logo-117100.

Sandvoss, Cornel. *Fans: The Mirror of Consumption*. Malden, MA: Polity Press, 2005.

Saurette, Paul, and Shane Gunster. "Ears Wide Shut: Epistemological Populism, Argutainment and Canadian Conservative Talk Radio." *Canadian Journal of Political Science / Revue Canadienne de Science Politique* 44, NO. 1 (2011): 195–218.

Scammell, Margaret. "The Wisdom of the War Room: US Campaigning and Americanization." *Media, Culture & Society* 20, NO. 2 (April 1, 1998): 251–75.

Schweizer, Peter. *Reagan's War: The Epic Story of His Forty Year Struggle and Final Triumph over Communism*. New York: Doubleday, 2002.

Sontag, Susan. "Notes on Camp." *Partisan Review* 31, NO. 4 (1964): 515–30.

Staal, Jonas. "Propaganda Art from the 20th to the 21st Century." Doctoral Thesis, Leiden University, 2018.

Staal, Jonas, and Marina Otero Verzier. *Steve Bannon: A Propaganda Retrospective By Jonas Staal*. Rotterdam: Het Nieuwe Instituut, 2018.

Taggart, Paul. *Populism*. Maidenhead: Open University Press, 2000.

The War Room. Documentary. Cyclone Films, McEttinger Films, Pennebaker Associates, 1993.

Thomas, Scott. *Designing Obama*. Post Press, 2009.

Urbinati, Nadia. "Between Hegemony and Distrust. Representative Democracy in the Internet Era." *Reset DOC* (blog), April 7, 2014. https://www.resetdoc.org/story/between-hegemony-and-distrust-representative-democracy-in-the-internet-era/.

Wiegand, Peter. "Clinton's 2016 Logo 'Fail' Not Likely to Lose Voters." Ideas & Insights | Ideas at Work. *Columbia Business School* (blog), April 14, 2015. https://www8.gsb.columbia.edu/articles/ideas-work/clinton-s-2016-logo-fail-not-likely-lose-voters.

Willsher, Kim. "The Family Name and Party Logo Have Gone but Can Marine Le Pen Detoxify Her Brand?" The Observer, January 7, 2017, sec. World news. https://www.theguardian.com/world/2017/jan/07marine-le-pen-front-national-revamp-french-presidential-election.

Zavattaro, Staci M. "Brand Obama: The Implications of a Branded President." Administrative Theory & Praxis 32, NO. 1 (2010): 123–28.

Zoonen, Liesbet van. *Entertaining the Citizen: When Politics and Popular Culture Converge*. Rowman & Littlefield, 2005.

CONCLUSIONS

Bridle, James. *New Dark Age: Technology and the End of the Future*. London: Verso Books, 2019.

Julier, Guy, and Anders V. Munch. "Introducing Design Culture." In *Design Culture: Objects and Approaches*, edited by Guy Julier, Anders V. Munch, Mads Nygaard Folkmann, Hans-Christian Jensen, and Niels Peter Skou, 1–7. London: Bloomsbury Publishing, 2019.

Laranjo, Francisco, ed. *Modes of Criticism: Design and Democracy*. Eindhoven: ONOMATOPEE, 2017.

Miessen, Markus, ed. *The Nightmare of Participation: (Crossbench Praxis as a Mode of Criticality)*. Cambridge, MA: Sternberg Press, 2011.

ACKNOWLEDGEMENTS

I wish to express my gratitude towards the institutions that supported this research and all the colleagues and professors with whom I have collaborated, exchanged ideas and sources of inspiration. In particular: my PhD supervisor Maddalena Dalla Mura; the external reviewers of my PhD thesis Francisco Laranjo, Marina Otero Verzier, and Letizia Bollini; the organizers of the seminar 'In Great Tempest' Pierfrancesco Califano, Alessandro Durighello, Serena De Mola, and Stefania D'Eri; the curator of the exhibition GEO—DESIGN: COVID-19 Martina Muzi.

Secondly, I would like to acknowledge the great support and confidence in my work provided by Jesse Muller, Natasha Rijkhoff, Silvio Lorusso and Michele Galluzzo, without which this book would not exist.

And lastly, I would like to thank my family for their constant and invaluable help: Marco, Carolina, Silvia and Matteo.

ABOUT THE AUTHOR

Noemi Biasetton is a design researcher, writer and editor based in Venice. She holds a BA in Design&Arts from Free University of Bozen-Bolzano, a MA in Information Design from Design Academy Eindhoven, and a Ph.D. in Design Sciences from Iuav University of Venice.

Her studies focus on design cultures and mediated forms of visual representation, with a specific interest in how these are deployed within the social and political dimension. Her practice includes the production of essays and articles, the organization of talks and lectures, and the contribution to research projects for cultural and educational institutions.

Since 2022 she curates the editorial project *Bookcloud* by bruno, which explores the relationship between design and literature through a series of printed conversations with researchers and practitioners from the fields of design, architecture, arts, and philosophy.

NOTES

NOTES

NOTES

NOTES

NOTES